Fetal Rights

POINT //// ////
\\\\\\\\ COUNTERPOINT ////

Affirmative Action
Amateur Athletics
American Military Policy
Animal Rights
Capital Punishment
DNA Evidence
Election Reform
Fetal Rights
Freedom of Speech
Gay Rights
Gun Control
Immigration Policy
Legalizing Marijuana
Mandatory Military Service
Media Bias
Mental Health Reform
Open Government
Physician-Assisted Suicide
Policing the Internet
Protecting Ideas
Religion in Public Schools
Rights of Students
Search and Seizure
Smoking Bans
The FCC and Regulating Indecency
The Right to Privacy
Tort Reform
Trial of Juveniles as Adults
The War on Terror
Welfare Reform

Fetal Rights

Alan Marzilli

SERIES CONSULTING EDITOR
Alan Marzilli, M.A., J.D.

CHELSEA HOUSE
PUBLISHERS
A Haights Cross Communications Company ®

Philadelphia

CHELSEA HOUSE PUBLISHERS

VP, New Product Development Sally Cheney
Director of Production Kim Shinners
Creative Manager Takeshi Takahashi
Manufacturing Manager Diann Grasse

Staff for FETAL RIGHTS

Executive Editor Lee Marcott
Editorial Assistant Carla Greenberg
Photo Editor Sarah Bloom
Production Editor Noelle Nardone
Series and Cover Designer Keith Trego
Layout 21st Century Publishing and Communications, Inc.

http://www.chelseahouse.com

First Printing

1 3 5 7 9 8 6 4 2

Library of Congress Cataloging-in-Publication Data

Marzilli, Alan.
   Fetal rights / Alan Marzilli.
      p. cm.—(Point/counterpoint)
   Includes bibliographical references and index.
   ISBN 0-7910-8643-7 (hard cover)
   1. Fetus—Legal status, laws, etc.—United States. 2. Unborn children (Law)—
United States. I. Title. II. Point-counterpoint (Philadelphia, Pa.)
KF481.M37 2005
342.7308'5—dc22

                                                    2005006533

All links and web addresses were checked and verified to be correct at the time of
publication. Because of the dynamic nature of the web, some addresses and links
may have changed since publication and may no longer be valid.

CONTENTS

Foreword   **6**

INTRODUCTION
A Fetus With No Rights or
an Unborn Child With Legal Rights?   **10**

POINT
An Embryo or Fetus Does Not Deserve
Legal Recognition as a Person   **20**

COUNTERPOINT
An Unborn Child Is a Person Who
Deserves Equal Protection
Under the Law   **38**

POINT
Fetal Homicide Laws Threaten
Women's Rights   **52**

COUNTERPOINT
Laws Must Protect Every Unborn
Child From Violence   **68**

POINT
Laws That Regulate the Conduct
of Pregnant Women Invade
Their Privacy   **80**

COUNTERPOINT
In Some Cases, the Law Must Protect
Unborn Children From Their
Mothers' Behavior   **100**

CONCLUSION
The Rise of Fetal Rights and Its
Impact on Bioethics and the
Abortion Debate   **116**

Notes   **128**

Resources   **134**

Elements of the Argument   **137**

Appendix: Beginning Legal Research   **140**

Index   **144**

Foreword
Alan Marzilli, M.A., J.D.
Durham, North Carolina

The debates presented in POINT/COUNTERPOINT are among the most interesting and controversial in contemporary American society, but studying them is more than an academic activity. They affect every citizen; they are the issues that today's leaders debate and tomorrow's will decide. The reader may one day play a central role in resolving them.

Why study both sides of the debate? It's possible that the reader will not yet have formed any opinion at all on the subject of this volume—but this is unlikely. It is more likely that the reader will already hold an opinion, probably a strong one, and very probably one formed without full exposure to the arguments of the other side. It is rare to hear an argument presented in a balanced way, and it is easy to form an opinion on too little information; these books will help to fill in the informational gaps that can never be avoided. More important, though, is the practical function of the series: Skillful argumentation requires a thorough knowledge of *both* sides—though there are seldom only two, and only by knowing what an opponent is likely to assert can one form an articulate response.

Perhaps more important is that listening to the other side sometimes helps one to see an opponent's arguments in a more human way. For example, Sister Helen Prejean, one of the nation's most visible opponents of capital punishment, has been deeply affected by her interactions with the families of murder victims. Seeing the families' grief and pain, she understands much better why people support the death penalty, and she is able to carry out her advocacy with a greater sensitivity to the needs and beliefs of those who do not agree with her. Her relativism, in turn, lends credibility to her work. Dismissing the other side of the argument as totally without merit can be too easy—it is far more useful to understand the nature of the controversy and the reasons *why* the issue defies resolution.

The most controversial issues of all are often those that center on a constitutional right. The Bill of Rights—the first ten amendments to the U.S. Constitution—spells out some of the most fundamental rights that distinguish the governmental system of the United States from those that allow fewer (or other) freedoms. But the sparsely worded document is open to interpretation, and clauses of only a few words are often at the heart of national debates. The Bill of Rights was meant to protect individual liberties; but the needs of some individuals clash with those of society as a whole, and when this happens someone has to decide where to draw the line. Thus the Constitution becomes a battleground between the rights of individuals to do as they please and the responsibility of the government to protect its citizens. The First Amendment's guarantee of "freedom of speech," for example, leads to a number of difficult questions. Some forms of expression, such as burning an American flag, lead to public outrage—but nevertheless are said to be protected by the First Amendment. Other types of expression that most people find objectionable, such as sexually explicit material involving children, are not protected because they are considered harmful. The question is not only where to draw the line, but how to do this without infringing on the personal liberties on which the United States was built.

The Bill of Rights raises many other questions about individual rights and the societal "good." Is a prayer before a high school football game an "establishment of religion" prohibited by the First Amendment? Does the Second Amendment's promise of "the right to bear arms" include concealed handguns? Is stopping and frisking someone standing on a corner known to be frequented by drug dealers a form of "unreasonable search and seizure" in violation of the Fourth Amendment? Although the nine-member U.S. Supreme Court has the ultimate authority in interpreting the Constitution, its answers do not always satisfy the public. When a group of nine people—sometimes by a five-to-four vote—makes a decision that affects the lives of hundreds of millions, public outcry can be expected. And the composition of the Court does change over time, so even a landmark decision is not guaranteed to stand forever. The limits of constitutional protection are always in flux.

These issues make headlines, divide courts, and decide elections. They are the questions most worthy of national debate, and this series aims to cover them as thoroughly as possible. Each volume sets out some of the key arguments surrounding a particular issue, even some views that most people consider extreme or radical—but presents a balanced perspective on the issue. Excerpts from the relevant laws and judicial opinions and references to central concepts, source material, and advocacy groups help the reader to explore the issues even further and to read "the letter of the law" just as the legislatures and the courts have established it.

It may seem that some debates—such as those over capital punishment and abortion, debates with a strong moral component—will never be resolved. But American history offers numerous examples of controversies that once seemed insurmountable but now are effectively settled, even if only on the surface. Abolitionists met with widespread resistance to their efforts to end slavery, and the controversy over that issue threatened to cleave the nation in two; but today public debate over the merits of slavery would be unthinkable, though racial inequalities still plague the nation. Similarly unthinkable at one time was suffrage for women and minorities, but this is now a matter of course. Distributing information about contraception once was a crime. Societies change, and attitudes change, and new questions of social justice are raised constantly while the old ones fade into irrelevancy.

Whatever the root of the controversy, the books in POINT/ COUNTERPOINT seek to explain to the reader the origins of the debate, the current state of the law, and the arguments on both sides. The goal of the series is to inform the reader about the issues facing not only American politicians, but all of the nation's citizens, and to encourage the reader to become more actively involved in resolving these debates, as a voter, a concerned citizen, a journalist, an activist, or an elected official. Democracy is based on education, and every voice counts—so every opinion must be an informed one.

———————————•————————————•————————————•———————————

This volume examines an issue that has received increasing attention due to high-profile events and its relationship to the national debate over the continued legality of abortion: the debate over what pro-choice advocates and many media outlets have termed "fetal rights," or what pro-life advocates think of as the rights of unborn children.

When Scott Peterson was accused of murdering his pregnant wife, prosecutors charged him with two murders—for the deaths of his wife and of his unborn son. Under California law, Peterson was convicted of murdering a "person" and a "fetus." However, under the laws of other jurisdictions, a similar crime could be prosecuted as the murders of two people or as one murder only. The case brought attention to the question of whether a fetus—or unborn child—is a person, and if so, whether he or she should have the full legal rights of a person who has already been born. The question touches many other areas of law, such as drug use by pregnant women. Pro-life and pro-choice activists have taken a keen interest because the resolution of the issues of personhood and rights could have a profound impact on the right to choose an abortion. The U.S. Supreme Court's *Roe* v. *Wade* decision, which established a woman's right to choose an abortion, relied on a finding that legal traditions did not recognize an embryo or a fetus as a person. By changing that legal tradition piece by piece, pro-life advocates hope that they can topple *Roe* v. *Wade*.

A Fetus With No Rights or an Unborn Child With Legal Rights?

O n Christmas Eve 2002, Laci Peterson disappeared from her California home. The attractive young woman was pregnant with her first child, whom she and her husband, Scott, had decided to name Conner. From the first days of the search for Laci, the case attracted national attention from a curious public, riveted by the attractive principal characters in the drama, Scott's admitted affair with a massage therapist, and speculation as to whether Scott was guilty of murder.

Several months later, the bodies of Laci and her unborn son washed ashore on San Francisco Bay about a mile apart from each other. After the discovery of the bodies, police arrested Scott Peterson and charged him with murder. Interest in the case continued to grow: The story splashed across nightly newscasts and tabloid newspapers, a television movie dramatized the events, and gamblers in Las Vegas casinos placed bets on whether Scott would be convicted.

Friends and family bring signs and flowers to the front yard of the Peterson home, Sunday, April 20, 2003, in Modesto, California. Scott Peterson was arrested for the murder of his wife, Laci, and was later convicted of her murder, as well as the murder of their unborn son, Conner.

Curiosity seekers were not the only people drawn into the Peterson case. The case sparked a serious political and cultural debate as well. Ultimately, a jury convicted Scott Peterson of two counts of murder, reflecting the fact that Laci was pregnant. During the trial, some news accounts noted that he was charged with murdering "Laci Peterson and her fetus," whereas others referred to "Laci Peterson and her unborn son, Conner." This difference in terminology might seem minor, but it symbolizes a national debate that has impassioned advocates on both sides. The debate between pro-life advocates and pro-choice advocates traditionally has focused on whether abortion should remain legal. In recent years, however, an increasingly hot topic of debate has been what pro-life advocates refer to as the rights of the unborn and what pro-choice advocates and many media outlets refer to as fetal rights.

[Author's note: The title of this book is not meant to convey support for the pro-choice position but merely reflects the widespread use of the term "fetal rights" by mainstream media, including a *Newsweek* cover story.]

The terms "embryo," "fetus," and "unborn child."

Pro-life advocates, who oppose abortion, generally believe that human life begins at conception. They argue that, when a woman becomes pregnant, she is carrying an unborn child, and because that child is a person like any person who has already been born, the unborn child deserves legal protection under the law. In 2004, a judge on a Florida appeals court expressed this viewpoint in a dissenting opinion. Criticizing the decision reached by the majority of the court—that an unborn child cannot have a legal guardian under Florida law—Judge Robert Pleus wrote:

> I would urge the Legislature to overturn this decision and affirm the fact that an unborn child is a person. Such action would be a clear and unambiguous acknowledgment of human life. I would submit further that defining "person" by

using terms such as "embryo" or "fetus" is confusing, outdated and meaningless . . . .

I have a new grandson. His name is Nicholas. His heart started beating a short time after conception and during the first trimester. At the end of the first trimester, or early in the second trimester, we were able to view a sonogram and deter-

FROM THE BENCH

The Complaint Against Scott Peterson

Stanislaus County prosecutors charged Scott Peterson with two counts of murder, alleging that he murdered both his wife, Laci, and his unborn son, Conner. California law recognizes the killing of Conner as murder, but note the difference in language: Laci is referred to as a "human being," and Conner is referred to as a "fetus."

On April 21, 2003, K. VELLA, STANISLAUS COUNTY DISTRICT ATTORNEY'S OFFICE, complains and alleges, upon information and belief, that said defendant(s) did commit the following crime(s) in the County of Stanislaus, State of California.

COUNT I: On or about and between December 23, 2002 and December 24, 2002, defendant did commit a felony, MURDER, violation of Section 187 of the California Penal Code, in that the defendant did willfully, unlawfully, and feloniously with malice aforethought murder Laci Denise Peterson, a human being. . . .

COUNT II: On or about and between December 23, 2002 and December 24, 2002, defendant did commit a felony, MURDER, violation of Section 187 of the California Penal Code, in that the defendant did willfully, unlawfully, and feloniously with malice aforethought murder Baby Conner Peterson, a fetus. . . .

It is further alleged as to Counts I & II, MURDER, the defendant committed more than one murder in the 1st or 2nd degree in this proceeding, and is a special circumstance within the meaning of [the] Penal Code. . . .

In November 2004, a jury convicted Peterson of first-degree murder in Laci's death and second-degree murder in Conner's death.

Source: Indictment of Scott Peterson (Stanislaus County, California, April 21, 2003).

mine that Nicholas was a boy. We have pictures of sonograms taken when Nicholas was only fourteen weeks old. You can see his head, his eyes, his hands and feet. You could tell he was alive because he moved his arms and legs. He was so strong you could watch him move his mother's pregnant belly. Before he was born, his parents placed a sign over his future crib. It read simply: "NICHOLAS." Nicholas now lives outside his mother's womb, but from the moment of his conception, Nicholas was a human life.[1]

In contrast, pro-choice advocates, who support a woman's right to choose an abortion, embrace the use of the terms "embryo" and "fetus," signifying their belief that a human being becomes a "person" or "child" with legal rights only after birth.

During gestation, or development in the uterus, several medical terms describe the developing life, depending on the level of development:

- A *zygote* is an egg that has been fertilized by a sperm cell. The zygote begins to grow and divide into new cells.

- The word *embryo* refers to the developing human being as it progresses through cell division and begins to take human shape. The embryonic stage lasts through the eighth week after fertilization, and it is during this period that harmful substances pose the greatest risk to development.

- The term *fetus* is used from the end of the embryonic period until birth.

The use of the term *unborn child* by pro-life advocates and the terms *embryo* and *fetus* by pro-choice advocates angers their adversaries. Orthodox priest Johannes Jacobse wrote, "Pro-choicers resist calling any unborn child a child at all. They prefer 'fetus' (Latin for little one) because it dehumanizes the aborted child."[2] On the other side of the debate, Rachel Roth criticizes the use of the term "unborn child" and referring to pregnant women as their "mothers." She argued that using such terms "suggests that all other aspect of [the woman's] identity cease to be relevant."[3] Because this book presents both sides of the debate and because no neutral language apparently exists, the terms *embryo* and *fetus* are used in chapters that cover opposition to rights for embryos and fetuses and the term *unborn child* is used in chapters that present support for rights for unborn children. The title of this book follows the use of the term "fetal rights" by many media outlets.

> • **Which term do you prefer, "fetus" or "unborn child"? Which term do you think a doctor would use? Which term do you think a pregnant woman would use?**

The legal debate.

In some ways, people who are involved in the debate over fetal rights, or rights of unborn children, are fighting a surrogate battle over abortion. Although candidates in local, state, and national elections try to attract voters by publicizing their stands on abortion, the legality of abortion is not a political question. State legislatures and the U.S. Congress cannot decide whether to legalize or outlaw abortion, because the U.S. Supreme Court ruled in the 1973 case *Roe* v. *Wade* that a woman has a constitutional right to choose an abortion, subject to certain limitations, and the U.S. Constitution trumps state and federal laws.

The scope of a woman's right to choose an abortion *is* a political question, however. Under *Roe* v. *Wade*, states have some right to regulate abortion after the first trimester, that is, after the first three months of pregnancy, which typically lasts nine months. States have even greater leeway to regulate abortion after viability, the time at which the developing human being is capable of survival if born prematurely. States typically ban postviability abortions, with exceptions for cases in which the woman's life or health is in jeopardy. At the time of the *Roe* v. *Wade* decision, the Court established the end of the second trimester as the approximate time of viability. As medical technology has moved the point of viability earlier, the Supreme Court has upheld the principle that a woman has the right to choose an abortion up until the time of viability:

> The soundness or unsoundness of that constitutional judgment in no sense turns on whether viability occurs at approximately 28 weeks, as was usual at the time of *Roe*, at 23 to 24 weeks, as it sometimes does today, or at some moment even slightly earlier in pregnancy, as it may if fetal respiratory capacity can somehow be enhanced in the future.[4]

Because pro-life advocates have been unable to persuade the Supreme Court to ban abortions before viability, wrote Rachel Roth in *Making Women Pay: The Hidden Cost of Fetal Rights*, they have adopted a two-part approach.[5] One plan of attack has been to try to enact stricter and stricter limitations on abortion, such as laws that require that a minor's parents be notified prior to her having an abortion. Another plan of attack has been to establish more rights for unborn children in other areas of the law. Pro-life advocates believe—and pro-choice advocates fear— that by legally establishing that an unborn child is a person, they can undermine an important premise of *Roe* v. *Wade*: that an unborn child is not a "person" protected by the Constitution, and therefore states are not obligated to protect its life, liberty, and property, as they are obligated to do for all "people" under the Fourteenth Amendment to the U.S. Constitution.

- **Do you support the right to choose an abortion? Do you think viability makes a difference?**

Pro-life advocates generally believe that life begins at conception, and therefore, they argue, an unborn child should have the same rights as any other person, from conception onward. The Court's opinion in *Roe* v. *Wade*—that an embryo or fetus is not a "person"—was based on analysis of legal history—laws and courts had almost uniformly considered a human being a "person" only after birth. The legal traditions cited by the Court had originated long before modern medical technology allowed doctors to understand embryonic and fetal development, let alone to watch a moving image of the fetus on an ultrasound machine, however.

Pro-life advocates have generally pushed for legal recognition of the personhood of unborn children in areas not directly related to abortion. Many Americans who support the right to choose an abortion do not take the extreme position advanced by some pro-choice advocates—that an embryo or fetus is a "clump of cells" and does not deserve any rights. More moderate pro-choice advocates are willing to acknowledge the humanity of an embryo or fetus but believe that a pregnant woman's rights are sometimes more important than an embryo or fetus's rights. In order to avoid widespread resistance, pro-life advocates have sought to establish the rights of unborn children in areas outside of the abortion context that are less likely to raise concerns among people with moderate pro-choice beliefs.

In 2002, the Bush administration expanded the State Children's Health Insurance Program (SCHIP), which enables states to provide health insurance to children from low-income families. The new regulation included unborn children among those who qualified for health coverage. Some pro-choice advocates reacted angrily to defining an embryo or fetus as a child, but the idea of providing prenatal care to low-income pregnant women was generally appealing to many people, including people who take moderate pro-choice positions. Other examples of laws not directly related to abortion include those that allow parents to sue for the wrongful death of an unborn child in cases of medical malpractice. Again, the idea of allowing parents to recover money for a mistake that leads to the stillbirth of an expected child does not raise the same public outcry as efforts to restrict abortions would.

As a result of the murders of Laci Peterson and—as defined by California law—her fetus, pro-life advocates gained momentum in their efforts to have Congress pass the Unborn Victims of Violence Act (UVVA), also known as Laci and Conner's Law. The heart-wrenching stories told by Laci Peterson's mother and numerous women who had been brutally attacked by people who sought to end their pregnancies swayed members of both Congress and the general public. Congress subsequently passed a law that recognized the murder of an unborn child under federal law.

• Should murder laws be the same in every state?

Under California law, prosecutors could, and did, charge Scott Peterson with the murder of a fetus. If Peterson had been charged under federal law (UVVA was enacted after Laci's death), he could have been charged with only one murder. It is important to note that most murders are prosecuted under state laws because federal murder laws apply only in certain circumstances, such as if the murder occurs on a military base or while someone is committing another federal crime, such as robbing a mail delivery. Therefore, even if "Laci and Conner's Law" had been in existence at the time of the murders, it would not have applied to Scott Peterson, who was charged under state law.

UVVA broke new ground in federal law. Although the Bush administration's SCHIP regulations recognized embryos and fetuses as "children," the regulations were not enacted by Congress, and therefore UVVA was the first time an act of Congress recognized embryos and fetuses as people. The law declared, "[The] term 'unborn child' means a child in utero, and the term 'child in utero' or 'child, who is in utero' means a member of the species homo sapiens, at any stage of development, who is carried in the womb."[6]

Pro-life advocates saw the passage of UVVA as a step in the right direction, whereas pro-choice advocates feared that the law chipped away at the foundation of a woman's right to choose abortion. The law certainly opens the door for legislation in other areas of intense public debate. A well-publicized incident soon after the passage of UVVA brought other longstanding fetal rights issues into the public's consciousness. Utah prosecutors charged Melissa Rowland with murder after one of her twins was stillborn, although she later pleaded guilty to the lesser charge of child endangerment.

Rowland reportedly had used cocaine during her pregnancy and refused to allow doctors to deliver the twins surgically, by cesarean section. The charges led to a clash between those feminists who believe that a woman has the right to make her own medical decisions regardless of harm to a fetus, and pro-life advocates, some of whom believe that the law should compel a woman to undergo medical procedures needed to preserve the life of an unborn child. The two sides also exchanged a war of words over whether a woman should face criminal charges for using drugs during pregnancy.

With the right to choose an abortion guaranteed by the U.S. Supreme Court's interpretation of the Constitution, pro-choice and pro-life advocates have begun intense debates over the rights of embryos and fetuses—or unborn children—outside of the abortion context. A primary area of contention is whether the law should recognize "personhood" before birth. Some specific questions include whether the murder of a pregnant woman should be considered two murders, whether courts should impose medical treatments necessary for a healthy delivery, and whether a woman should be prosecuted for using drugs while pregnant.

An Embryo or Fetus Does Not Deserve Legal Recognition as a Person

In December 1988, Nancy Klein was involved in a serious car accident on Long Island, New York. The icy wreck left her in a coma, and doctors were not sure whether she would ever regain consciousness. At the time of the accident, Klein was almost three months pregnant, and the doctors suggested to her husband that they perform an abortion. In their opinion, the abortion would reduce the physical demands on her body and improve her chances of survival.

Because consent is needed for an abortion and Nancy was unconscious, her husband, Martin, was appointed as her legal guardian so that he could give the necessary consent. Two anti-abortion activists, John Short and John Broderick, convinced a judge to appoint them as guardians for the fetus, even though they did not know the Kleins. This set off a legal battle that made its way through several courts and included an appeal to the U.S.

Supreme Court. Writer Catherine Whitney commented, "While the nation watched in horror, the embattled husband was subjected to numerous stalling tactics, even though every moment his wife remained in a coma made the decision more critical."[7]

> • **Should a stranger be allowed to make decisions for an unborn child? For a five-year-old child?**

Martin Klein eventually prevailed in court, and doctors performed the abortion. "Soon after the abortion, I regained consciousness. The pregnancy [had] put a lot of strain on my body," Nancy Klein told an audience at a pro-choice gathering on Long Island in 2003.[8] Her accident had left her with serious disabilities, but she had regained her ability to think and speak, and she has become a spokesperson and a symbol for the pro-choice movement. A television movie, *Absolute Strangers*, chronicled her story. The movie's title came from a court ruling that overturned the men's guardianship and noted that they were absolute strangers to Nancy Klein.

To pro-choice advocates, the question is not the men's relationship with Nancy Klein, but whether a fetus should be appointed a guardian at all. Appointing a legal guardian to a fetus assumes that it is a "person," legally speaking, and most pro-choice advocates reject this designation. Their fear is that legal recognition of an embryo or fetus as a person under law would undermine abortion rights, as well as women's ability to make other decisions regarding pregnancy. In recent years, embryos and fetuses have been gaining recognition as "people" in various legal contexts, and the pro-choice movement has redoubled its efforts to combat this trend.

Life begins at birth.

In the landmark 1973 *Roe* v. *Wade* case, which established the constitutional right to choose an abortion, abortion rights activists tried to persuade the U.S. Supreme Court to adopt the legal position that life begins at birth. The Court avoided the

(continued on page 24)

Legal Traditions of Personhood Influenced
Roe v. *Wade* Decision

In its landmark 1973 decision that recognized the constitutional right to choose an abortion, the U.S. Supreme Court was influenced by legal traditions, which generally did not recognize an embryo or fetus as a "person," in finding that the U.S. Constitution's protection of "life, liberty, and the pursuit of happiness" did not apply to an embryo or fetus.

It is undisputed that at common law, abortion performed before "quickening"—the first recognizable movement of the fetus in utero, appearing usually from the 16th to the 18th week of pregnancy—was not an indictable offense. The absence of a common-law crime for pre-quickening abortion appears to have developed from a confluence of earlier philosophical, theological, and civil and canon law concepts of when life begins. These disciplines variously approached the question in terms of the point at which the embryo or fetus became "formed" or recognizably human, or in terms of when a "person" came into being, that is, infused with a "soul" or "animated." A loose consensus evolved in early English law that these events occurred at some point between conception and live birth. This was "mediate animation." Although Christian theology and the canon law came to fix the point of animation at 40 days for a male and 80 days for a female, a view that persisted until the 19th century, there was otherwise little agreement about the precise time of formation or animation. There was agreement, however, that prior to this point the fetus was to be regarded as part of the mother, and its destruction, therefore, was not homicide. Due to continued uncertainty about the precise time when animation occurred, to the lack of any empirical basis for the 40–80-day view, and perhaps to Aquinas' definition of movement as one of the two first principles of life, Bracton focused upon quickening as the critical point. The significance of quickening was echoed by later common-law scholars and found its way into the received common law in this country. . . .

It should be sufficient to note briefly the wide divergence of thinking on this most sensitive and difficult question. There has always been strong support for the view that life does not begin until live birth. This was the belief of the Stoics. It appears to be the predominant, though not the unanimous, attitude of the Jewish faith. It may be taken to represent also the position of a large segment of the Protestant community, insofar as that can be ascertained; organized groups that have taken a formal position on the abortion issue have generally regarded abortion as a matter for the conscience of the individual and her family. As we have noted, the common law found greater significance in quickening. Physicians and their scientific colleagues have regarded that event with less interest and have tended to focus either upon conception, upon live birth, or upon the interim point at which the fetus becomes "viable," that is, potentially able to live outside the mother's womb, albeit with artificial aid. Viability is usually placed at about seven months (28 weeks) but may occur earlier, even at 24 weeks. The Aristotelian theory of "mediate animation," that held sway throughout the Middle Ages and the Renaissance in Europe, continued to be official Roman Catholic dogma until the 19th century....

In areas other than criminal abortion, the law has been reluctant to endorse any theory that life, as we recognize it, begins before live birth or to accord legal rights to the unborn except in narrowly defined situations and except when the rights are contingent upon live birth. For example, the traditional rule of tort law denied recovery for prenatal injuries even though the child was born alive. That rule has been changed in almost every jurisdiction. In most States, recovery is said to be permitted only if the fetus was viable, or at least quick, when the injuries were sustained, though few courts have squarely so held. In a recent development, generally opposed by the commentators, some States permit the parents of a stillborn child to maintain an action for wrongful death because of prenatal injuries. Such an action, however, would appear to be one to vindicate the parents' interest and is thus consistent with the view that the fetus, at most, represents only the potentiality of life. Similarly, unborn children have been recognized as acquiring rights or interests by way of inheritance or other devolution of property, and have been represented by guardians ad litem. Perfection of the interests involved, again, has generally been contingent upon live birth. In short, the unborn have never been recognized in the law as persons in the whole sense.

Source: *Roe* v. *Wade*, 410 U.S. 113 (citations and footnotes omitted).

(continued from page 21)

question. Justice Harry Blackmun wrote, "We need not resolve the difficult question of when life begins. When those trained in the respective disciplines of medicine, philosophy, and theology are unable to arrive at any consensus, the judiciary, at this point in the development of man's knowledge, is not in a position to speculate as to the answer." [9]

In the decades since that decision, pro-choice advocates have steadfastly maintained that life begins at birth, for this theory of life is vital to preservation of abortion rights. In *Roe* v. *Wade*, the Supreme Court acknowledged that "if this suggestion of personhood [of the fetus] is established, the [case for abortion rights], of course, collapses, for the fetus' right to life would then be guaranteed specifically by the [Fourteenth] Amendment [to the U.S. Constitution]." [10] Therefore, pro-choice advocates realize that, to preserve abortion rights, they must discredit the belief that life begins before birth or at least must keep the question open.

> • **When do you think life begins? Do you think someone becomes a person sometime after life begins?**

The debate over the beginning of life in the aftermath of *Roe* v. *Wade* is best characterized as a standoff, with each side refusing to blink. The most common pro-life position is that life begins at conception—when a sperm cell fertilizes an egg cell, resulting in a single-celled fertilized egg called a zygote. Although they do not deny that the resulting zygote is "human," most pro-choice advocates argue that the zygote is not a form of life but rather represents the potential for human life. Feminist Joyce Arthur wrote, "A fertilized egg . . . [represents] a *potential*, not an actual human being. It's a worn cliché, but it bears repeating—an acorn isn't an oak tree and the egg you had for breakfast isn't a chicken." [11]

The transformation from a zygote to a baby taking his or her first breath is a complicated process. When the human egg is fertilized by a sperm cell, the resulting zygote has a complete set of DNA, which contains all of the genetic information needed for the zygote to develop into an adult person. Certain conditions are also necessary for the development to take place. The egg must divide successfully, attach to the woman's uterus within 72 hours, and then receive the proper nutrition through the placenta. Often, a fertilized egg does not lead to a live birth because it implants in the woman's fallopian tube or elsewhere outside the uterus. The resulting pregnancy, called "ectopic," cannot be carried to term successfully and also can pose a great threat to the woman's life, frequently necessitating surgery. Sometimes, the developing embryo or fetus is miscarried because of a genetic abnormality that makes a live birth impossible. Such genetically induced miscarriages can take place well into the first trimester, that is, up until the third month of pregnancy.

Because the question of when life begins has remained controversial, some pro-choice advocates have attempted to reframe the question. Rather than asking when life begins, wrote Vanessa Cullins, medical director of Planned Parenthood Federation of America, "The really hot question is, 'When does being a person begin?' Most medical authorities and Planned Parenthood agree that it starts when a baby takes its first breath."[12]

Legal traditions support birth as the beginning of personhood.

The right to choose an abortion established by the 1973 *Roe* v. *Wade* decision has two basic components: first, that women have a constitutional right to privacy that includes the right to make decisions about abortion, and second, that an embryo or fetus is not a "person" whose life, liberty, and property are guaranteed constitutional protection. Pro-life advocates have widely criticized the Supreme Court for "inventing" the constitutional right to privacy—legal scholar Robert Bork has written that the opinion contains "not one line of explanation, not one sentence that qualifies as a legal argument," on the subject.[13] Justice Blackmun's opinion in *Roe* v. *Wade,* however, offered historical justification

Abortion laws toughen in many states

Many states have made abortions less accessible with tougher laws such as mandatory waiting periods and parental notification for minors.

States that require a waiting period

Nineteen states enforce a required waiting period before an abortion, most of them for at least 24 hours. Georgia, Minnesota, Arizona and Washington have bills pending that would require waiting periods.

States that do not require parental involvement

All but eight states have laws regarding parental notification for minors. Thirty-one enforce parental consent or notification before a minor can have an abortion, and 11 have laws that are not in effect.

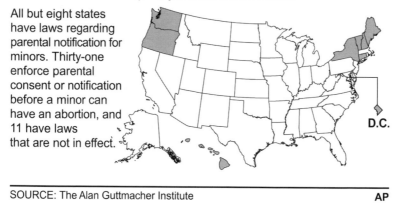

SOURCE: The Alan Guttmacher Institute

AP

The maps above illustrate which states have laws that place restrictions on access to abortion. Nineteen states require that a woman who wishes to have an abortion must wait for a specified period after seeing a doctor to get the abortion. Thirty-one states require that the parents of a minor who wishes to have an abortion must be notified.

for its conclusion that an embryo or fetus is not, legally speaking, a person. He wrote:

> Parties challenging state abortion laws . . . claim that most state laws were designed solely to protect the woman . . . . There is some scholarly support for this view of original purpose. The few state courts called upon to interpret their laws in the late 19th and early 20th centuries did focus on the State's interest in protecting the woman's health rather than in preserving the embryo and fetus. Proponents of this view point out that in many States, including Texas, by statute or judicial interpretation, the pregnant woman herself could not be prosecuted for self-abortion or for cooperating in an abortion performed upon her by another.
>
> They claim that adoption of the "quickening" distinction through received common law and state statutes tacitly recognizes the greater health hazards inherent in late abortion and impliedly repudiates the theory that life begins at conception.[14]

Today, four of the nine Supreme Court Justices oppose the constitutional right to choose abortion—arguing that the right is not supported by legal traditions—but pro-choice advocates have sought to use similar historical arguments to bolster their position that an embryo or fetus is not a person. Historian Barbara Duden wrote, "The prenatal person in the womb that we talk about today stands on shaky juridical ground," noting that under Roman law, damages to a pregnant woman were treated similarly to damages to a cow carrying calves.[15] Noting that English jurist William Blackstone's attempts to classify a fetus as a person conflicted with both medieval and contemporary church law, she concluded, "The natural person whose integrity and freedom can be protected by a legal system appears only in modern times, and it took centuries before this kind of person was first placed within the womb."[16]

• **Should a court made up of nine people decide a question as important as the legality of abortion?**

Pro-choice journalist Janet Hadley noted that the legal basis for denying full personhood status to an embryo or fetus lies in the inseparable connection with the woman up until the time of birth. She wrote, "Traditionally, the *law* pinpoints birth—the observable separation of mother and infant—as the moment when personhood begins. From then onwards, all persons must be considered of equal value before the law." [17]

FROM THE BENCH

Justice Stevens: No Secular Reason for Declaring That Life Begins at Conception.

Dissenting from the U.S. Supreme Court's decision in *Webster*, Justice John Paul Stevens argued that the legislature had no secular (nonreligious) reason for declaring that life begins at conception and that the law violated the First Amendment's prohibition on the Establishment of Religion. In his view—not shared by other members of the court—declaring that life begins at conception is no different than a legislature adopting the ancient views of St. Thomas Aquinas.

If the views of St. Thomas were held as widely today as they were in the Middle Ages, and if a state legislature were to enact a statute prefaced with a "finding" that female life begins 80 days after conception and male life begins 40 days after conception, I have no doubt that this Court would promptly conclude that such an endorsement of a particular religious tenet is violative of the Establishment Clause.

In my opinion the difference between that hypothetical statute and Missouri's preamble reflects nothing more than a difference in theological doctrine. The preamble to the Missouri statute endorses the theological position that there is the same secular interest in preserving the life of a fetus during the first 40 or 80 days of pregnancy as there is after viability—indeed, after the time when the fetus has become a "person" with legal rights protected by the Constitution. To sustain that position as a matter of law, I believe Missouri has the burden of identifying the secular interests

In the century leading up to the *Roe* v. *Wade* decision, American courts began to recognize some rights of embryos and fetuses, but these rights could only be exercised by a person who was born alive—the so-called "born alive" rule. In *Making Women Pay*, Rachel Roth cited an 1887 Connecticut decision that allowed a person to inherit property from another person who died after the first person was conceived but before he or she was born, as well as a 1946 decision that allowed someone to sue for injuries caused while he or she was still in utero. Roth noted that these decisions "were narrow exceptions to the general

that differentiate the first 40 days of pregnancy from the period immediately before or after fertilization when, as *Griswold* and related cases establish, the Constitution allows the use of contraceptive procedures to prevent potential life from developing into full personhood. Focusing our attention on the first several weeks of pregnancy is especially appropriate because that is the period when the vast majority of abortions are actually performed.

As a secular matter, there is an obvious difference between the state interest in protecting the freshly fertilized egg and the state interest in protecting a 9-month-gestated, fully sentient fetus on the eve of birth. There can be no interest in protecting the newly fertilized egg from physical pain or mental anguish, because the capacity for such suffering does not yet exist; respecting a developed fetus, however, that interest is valid. In fact, if one prescinds the theological concept of ensoulment—or one accepts St. Thomas Aquinas' view that ensoulment does not occur for at least 40 days—a State has no greater secular interest in protecting the potential life of an embryo that is still "seed" than in protecting the potential life of a sperm or an unfertilized ovum.

Source: *Webster* v. *Reproductive Health Services*, 492 U.S. 490 (1989) (Stevens, J., concurring in part and dissenting in part).

rule," with the general rule being the "Anglo-American legal tradition of treating a fetus as part of pregnant woman."[18]

Pro-choice advocates also point out that, even after the *Roe* v. *Wade* decision, American law has not recognized the personhood of an embryo or fetus. In written comments that opposed the Bush administration's proposal to expand SCHIP to include embryos and fetuses, the National Abortion Rights Action League (NARAL) argued:

> No federal law to our knowledge gave legal rights and benefits to an embryo or fetus as an individual. That is, an embryo or fetus is not given a social security number; it is not a Medicaid beneficiary; pregnant women do not receive an exemption on their income taxes for the embryo or fetus; census-takers count only born individuals; and, most pertinently, Congress did not designate embryos or fetuses as beneficiaries for the SCHIP program.[19]

Although NARAL and other pro-choice groups accused the Bush administration of "pushing a political agenda rather than a public health concern,"[20] the Department of Health and Human Services adopted the regulation.

Defining birth as the beginning of personhood protects women's rights.

The primary reason that pro-choice advocates are opposed to laws that endow an embryo or fetus with rights from conception onward is that such laws threaten women's rights. In a policy statement, the Planned Parenthood Federation of America maintained, "To impose a law defining a fetus as a 'person,' granting it rights equal to or superior to a woman's—a thinking, feeling, conscious human being—is arrogant and absurd. It only serves to diminish women."[21]

Legal recognition of the embryo or fetus as a person could eventually limit a woman's legal ability to choose abortion, to use certain forms of birth control, and to make medical decisions regarding pregnancy. One such decision is whether or not to have a cesarean section, or C-section, in which the baby is delivered surgically by cutting through the belly. In some pregnancies, when doctors determine that a natural delivery would pose risks to the baby, they recommend a C-section. The procedure is a major operation, however, one that not every woman wants to undergo.

During the presidency of George W. Bush, several legal developments have, in pro-choice advocates' opinion, threatened women's legal rights.

- In 2002, the U.S. Department of Health and Human Services expanded SCHIP to include embryos and fetuses in its definition of children who are eligible for health care coverage.

- The Partial Birth Abortion Ban Act of 2003, a federal law, outlawed one type of abortion procedure. Although the U.S. Supreme Court has not ruled on the validity of this law, lower federal courts have blocked its enforcement.

- The Unborn Victims of Violence Act of 2004, a federal law, allows embryos or fetuses to be considered murder victims—although abortion procedures are specifically exempted.

- In Florida, President Bush's brother, Governor Jeb Bush, unsuccessfully sought to have a legal guardian appointed to represent the rights of a fetus carried by a woman with a mental disability.

Although none of these legal developments has, by itself, outlawed abortion, many pro-choice advocates fear that, taken together, the laws weaken the right to choose an abortion. In a newspaper editorial, Professor Lynn Morgan and bioethicist Monica Casper called pro-life advocates "zealots," calling their efforts to enact laws to recognize the personhood of a fetus a "stealth campaign" advancing on multiple fronts.[22] They warned, "Don't be surprised to awaken one day to hear that a 'Fetal Protection Act' has been passed or a 'Fetal Protection Agency' formed."[23] Roth noted that the development of fetal rights in various contexts sends a message to women that they are "not entitled to the same respect and security as other members of society [and] that their status as potential childbearers reduces them to a kind of second-class citizenship."[24]

Many pro-choice advocates and feminists characterize pro-life advocates as being generally opposed to women's rights. British journalist Janet Hadley wrote, "Beneath the cloak of the moral issue"—whether or not an embryo or fetus is a person—"many opponents of abortion rights share deep-seated hostility to women's rights in general."[25] Indeed, many pro-life politicians are generally conservative politically and have opposed women's rights legislation, such as stronger sexual harassment and employment discrimination laws.

Morgan and Casper blasted the Bush administration for its changes to the SCHIP program because the changes provided for the health of the embryo or fetus but not for the woman from whom the embryo or fetus is inseparable until birth. They wrote:

> The proposed change would grant medical coverage to low-income women only when they were pregnant, only because they were pregnant, and only to treat the fetus rather than the woman herself. If the change were enacted, would SCHIP deny coverage to a pregnant woman who got high blood pressure or diabetes? Would it pay for miscarriage? Would it cover the costs of hospitalization for pre-term labor? How, exactly, would the program define the point at which care of the fetus would stop and care to the pregnant woman would begin? Is women's health only interesting to the medical establishment and the federal government when fetuses are at risk? It is an affront to American women to suggest that the government would extend certain rights and privileges

to fetuses, even when the women in whose bodies they reside are not entitled to those same rights and privileges. It would be much more sensible to expand health insurance coverage to all women of reproductive age, and to pregnant women in particular.[26]

Although most pro-life advocates believe that life begins at conception and that this conclusion has support in science, law, and religious belief, they also have to acknowledge that the issue remains controversial, with many people believing that life begins at some other point. Therefore, a frequent pro-life position is that because there is no way of being certain when life begins, the question must be resolved in favor of the fetus, to be on the safe side. Pro-choice advocates have a different viewpoint on how to resolve the uncertainty. Feminist Joyce Arthur wrote, "Biology, medicine, law, philosophy, and theology have no consensus on the issue, and neither does society as a whole. . . . [Thus,] we must give the benefit of the doubt to women, who are indisputable human beings with rights."[27]

> • **Do you think that restrictions on abortion are religiously based?**

As a fallback position, many supporters of abortion rights maintain that, even if the law recognizes the personhood of a fetus, the law could also recognize a limited right to abortion. Hadley wrote, "I do not discount the question of the fetus's moral value as a potential person, but for me, attributing a potential moral status to the fetus does not instantly close down the argument [that women should have a right to choose abortion]."[28] She believes that whatever rights the embryo or fetus had would have to be balanced against the woman's rights in determining whether to carry the embryo or fetus to term. In her opinion, "women themselves, because of their unique relationship to the fetus . . . are more likely to make a morally informed judgment than anyone else about an abortion."[29]

Feminist Eileen McDonagh has taken a more radical approach. Arguing in favor of abortion rights, she asserted that, if a fetus is given rights as a person, the fetus also must be held to the same standards of conduct as people who have already been born. In her view, the fetus is actually harming the woman by causing significant physiological changes, such as changes in blood flow and the growth of a placenta. Therefore, McDonagh said, if a state views a fetus as a person, then "the state is under an obligation not just to protect the fetus, but to stop the fetus from causing harm, just as the state would stop a born person [from assaulting the woman]."[30] The problem with the fetal rights debate, in McDonagh's view, is that "pro-life people [assert] that the fetus should have the same protection as a born person . . . [but] currently the fetus has more protection than a born person."[31]

> • **Should a pregnant woman have legal protections from her unborn child? Do illnesses caused by pregnancy justify abortion?**

Defining conception as the start of life is too extreme.

Many pro-choice advocates would prefer to have birth fixed as the legal beginning of personhood. As the pro-life movement gains inroads into American law, however, some pro-choice advocates might be willing to concede an earlier start of personhood, such as viability, after which abortion is already strictly regulated. In contrast, accepting conception as the beginning of life would lead to a great many consequences

In *Hard Choices, Lost Voices*, law Professor Donald Judges examined arguments on both sides of the abortion debate. He pointed out that one flaw in defining a fertilized egg as a living person is that "most fertilized eggs spontaneously abort," meaning that a majority of lives end before anyone ever notices that they began.[32] Although supporters of the belief that life begins at conception frequently say that choosing any other time as the start of life is arbitrary, Judges noted that, because "a fertilized egg represents only the *potential* for developing into a baby," it follows that "if it is murder to destroy a fertilized egg, then the destruction of sperm cells or unfertilized eggs would also seem to be murder, as they too are only the potentiality of life." [33]

Definition of conception as the beginning of life raises the practical consideration of how the legal system can accommodate the rights of the many thousands of frozen embryos created through in vitro fertilization (IVF) and stored for later attempts at pregnancy. Catherine Whitney noted in 1991 that more than 4,000 frozen embryos were being stored (the number is much higher today) and that many of these frozen embryos enjoyed some form of protection under state laws, some which she characterized as "absurd." She singled out a 1986 Louisiana law that "defines a frozen embryo as a juridical person, giving it full legal status and the right to be represented by a lawyer. That's quite a stretch for four to eight cells!" [34] Court cases have addressed parents' battles over the custody of frozen embryos, and public policy debates have questioned the ethics of using unwanted embryos for research purposes.

In a well-publicized 1992 decision, the Supreme Court of Tennessee, was faced with a "custody" battle between a divorced couple over several frozen embryos created with their sperm and egg cells through IVF. Central to the disposition of the case was the question of personhood, and the court considered arguments at both ends of the spectrum. Some parties to the lawsuit argued that, from the moment of conception, a fertilized egg, and therefore a multicelled embryo, deserved legal recognition as a person. Other parties argued that the frozen embryos in question should be treated as a form of property, as would other forms of human tissue, such as donated blood or organs. In the middle was a position described by the court as follows:

> It holds that the preembryo deserves respect greater than that accorded to human tissue but not the respect accorded to actual

persons. The preembryo is due greater respect than other human tissue because of its potential to become a person and because of its symbolic meaning for many people. Yet, it should not be treated as a person, because it has not yet developed the features of personhood, is not yet established as developmentally individual, and may never realize its biologic potential.[35]

The court adopted this compromise position to determine the legal status of frozen embryos created during the IVF process, holding that the embryos were not a form of life but instead represented a potential human life. The court wrote, "We conclude that preembryos are not, strictly speaking, either 'persons' or 'property,' but occupy an interim category that entitles them to special respect because of their potential for human life."[36]

With the increased availability of IVF, the number of frozen embryos has skyrocketed. In 2002, the U.S. Department of Health and Human Services announced the availability of nearly one million dollars in federal funding to promote "embryo adoption," reporting that more than 100,000 frozen embryos were in storage in the United States.[37] Some commentators have questioned how the court system could possibly treat each as an individual due a "day in court," accusing the Bush administration of pushing a pro-life agenda by viewing the use of a frozen embryo by an unrelated couple as an adoption rather than as a donation of property.

Jeffrey Kahn, director of the Center for Bioethics at the University of Minnesota, places the number of frozen embryos at more than 200,000. He characterized the Bush administration's support of "embryo adoption" as a "step away from couples controlling the fate of their embryos, and toward viewing embryos as needing government protection and the help of groups that seek to 'place' them with caring families. The way we're heading, it's a short step to lab freezers being called orphanages, and social workers assigned to look after the interests of their frozen charges."[38] To Kahn, such a result is impractical and undesirable.

Even some of the fiercest opponents of abortion rights have endorsed a viewpoint that life does not necessarily begin at conception. A topic of intense public debate has been medical research on embryos, or stem cell research. Most pro-life organizations and politicians have opposed such research, but Utah Senator Orrin Hatch—a longtime abortion foe—has spoken in favor of it. He distinguishes stem cell research from abortion by stating his belief that "life begins in a mother's womb." [39] Although Hatch's view leaves room for stem cell research, contraception, and IVF, it is of course incompatible with abortion and therefore unlikely to win acceptance among pro-choice groups. Rebecca Farmer, press secretary of the National Organization for Women (NOW), accused Hatch and other senators who share his viewpoint of sexism. She argued that they support stem cell research only because men stand to gain from any cures developed: "These Senators clearly demonstrate that when it is in men's interest to promote certain reproductive health policies but continue to deny others to women, they will do so without hesitation." [40]

Summary

Many pro-choice advocates recognize that an embryo or fetus is a developing human being but argue that life, and therefore legal recognition as a person, does not begin until birth. They argue that granting legal rights at conception would interfere with a woman's right to choose an abortion and to make her own medical decisions. In addition, they maintain, such a definition is impractical because of the large number of miscarriages that occur after conception and the growing number of frozen embryos whose legal status is uncertain.

An Unborn Child Is a Person Who Deserves Equal Protection Under the Law

In 1996, Roberto was diagnosed with a large mass in his lung. The growth of the mass posed a great threat to his heart. Surgery would not be easy because Roberto had not yet been born! Months before his due date, his mother's doctor discovered the mass with an ultrasound machine, which is used to produce an image of the fetus. A short time later, doctors discovered that the mass had indeed caused a life-threatening heart condition. Within days, the expectant parents had flown from Florida to Philadelphia, where the Children's Hospital offered a new surgical technique that would allow doctors to remove the mass and then return Roberto to the womb.

Doctors made an incision in the uterus, lifted Roberto's chest and arm through the opening, and successfully removed a mass that was almost as large as Roberto's chest cavity. They then replaced Roberto in the uterus, closed the incision, and arranged for the expectant mother to be closely monitored to prevent a dangerously early delivery. Roberto was born three months later—five weeks before his original due date but far enough into his mother's pregnancy to allow for a healthy childhood.

To pro-life advocates, stories such as this one serve as illustrations of their belief that every life, at every stage of development, is valuable. Although Roberto's diagnosis would have been hopeless years earlier, medical technology has made it possible to treat a human fetus as a "second patient." Medical technology has also allowed doctors and scientists to learn more about how a human being develops. Most pro-life advocates view human development as a continuous process from conception until natural death. In the 1980s, pro-life advocates used the film *The Silent Scream*, which depicts the abortion of an 11-week fetus, to show that, even at this early stage of prenatal development, an unborn child has many of the characteristics of a person.

The dominant pro-life viewpoint goes beyond appearances and looks at genetics. Because the fertilized egg has all of the genetic information needed to develop into adulthood, it is argued, life begins at conception, and therefore all of the legal rights of personhood should also begin at conception. Contrasting with the pro-choice view that recognition of the personhood of an unborn child diminishes the rights of women is a strong belief that failure to recognize personhood threatens the rights of unborn children. During the presidency of George W. Bush, pro-life advocates have made many inroads into changing the legal definition of a "person" to include unborn children.

Life begins at conception.

The Roman Catholic Church, which opposes both abortion and artificial birth control, teaches that life begins at conception, and many pro-life advocates take a similar stand based upon their own religious beliefs. In 1995, Pope John Paul II wrote:

> Many biblical passages . . . respectfully and lovingly speak of
> conception . . . and of the intimate connection between the
> initial moment of life and the action of God the Creator. . . .
> How can anyone think that even a single moment of this
> marvelous process of the unfolding of life could be separated
> from the wise and loving work of the Creator, and left prey to
> human caprice?[41]

Because the U.S. Constitution's prohibition of the establishment of religion has been interpreted to require a separation of church and state, many pro-life advocates have shied away from religious arguments about the beginning of life and instead focus on secular justifications for the recognition that human life begins at conception.

Another important document of the Catholic faith noted that setting conception as the beginning of life is based on sound science. In 1987, the Sacred Congregation for the Doctrine of the Faith noted in *The Gift of Life* that the Roman Catholic Church's teaching that "from the time that the ovum is fertilized . . . it is . . . a new human being with his own growth," has scientific support.[42] The Congregation's report continued, "Human biological science [recognizes] that in the zygote resulting from fertilization the biological identity of a new human individual is already constituted."[43]

The Congregation acknowledged that no scientific experiment could be conducted to determine the theological question of when the human soul develops. Ancient church teachings placed the development of the soul at a time much later than conception. St. Augustine wrote in the fourth century that "hominization," or development into a "fully formed human," occurred 40 days after conception for males and 80 days after conception for females.[44] In the thirteenth century, St. Thomas Aquinas—following the view of Greek philosopher Aristotle—taught that "infusion of the human soul" occurred between 40 and 80 days after conception. The Congregation maintained that general principles of developmental biology show that human development is a continuous process from conception until death, and because no sudden change takes place, "a personal presence" must be present at conception, asking rhetorically, "How could a human individual not be a human person?"[45]

The quoted passage addresses an argument frequently advanced by pro-choice advocates—that an embryo or fetus is human but is not yet a person. The pro-choice arguments sometimes pick another point in development, such as the development of a heartbeat, the detection of brain activity, or the ability to feel pain, as the start of "personhood." A point commonly cited as the start of personhood is the point of viability—when the unborn child would be able to survive outside the mother's womb if he or she was born. Generally, doctors consider the point of viability to be about 24 weeks into the pregnancy. Viability has important legal significance because the Supreme Court ruled in *Roe* v. *Wade* and later cases that states have a greater interest in protecting the lives of unborn children after they reach the point of viability.

- **Do physical characteristics such as arms and legs define whether a living being is a person?**

Pro-life advocates reject this distinction, saying that at no point is the interest in preserving life any greater than at any other point, because human development is a continuous process. Law and philosophy professor Francis Beckwith wrote in a publication of the Center for Bioethics and Human Dignity:

> From a strictly scientific point of view, there is no doubt that individual human life begins at conception and does not end until natural death. At the moment of conception, when sperm and ovum cease to exist as individual entities, a new being with its own genetic code comes into existence. All that is [needed] for its development is food, water, air, and an environment conducive to its survival.[46]

Ronald Reagan's "Personhood Proclamation"

In 1988, just before leaving office, Ronald Reagan issued a presidential proclamation to declare that unborn children are people who deserve the full protection of the law. Because the proclamation directly conflicted with the Supreme Court's abortion rulings, his proclamation does not have legal weight.

One of [the] unalienable rights, as the Declaration of Independence affirms so eloquently, is the right to life. In the 15 years since the Supreme Court's decision in *Roe* v. *Wade*, however, America's unborn have been denied their right to life....

That right to life belongs equally to babies in the womb, babies born handicapped, and the elderly or infirm. That we have killed the unborn for 15 years does not nullify this right, nor could any number of killings ever do so. The unalienable right to life is found not only in the Declaration of Independence but also in the Constitution that every President is sworn to preserve, protect, and defend. Both the Fifth and Fourteenth Amendments guarantee that no person shall be deprived of life without due process of law.

All medical and scientific evidence increasingly affirms that children before birth share all the basic attributes of human personality—that they in fact are persons. Modern medicine treats unborn children as patients. Yet, as the Supreme Court itself has noted, the decision in *Roe* v. *Wade* rested upon an earlier state of medical technology. The law of the land in 1988 should recognize all of the medical evidence....

NOW, THEREFORE, I, Ronald Reagan, President of the United States of America, by virtue of the authority vested in me by the Constitution and the laws of the United States, do hereby proclaim and declare the unalienable personhood of every American, from the moment of conception until natural death, and I do proclaim, ordain, and declare that I will take care that the Constitution and laws of the United States are faithfully executed for the protection of America's unborn children.

Source: Presidential Proclamation No. 5761 (January 14, 1988), reprinted at *http://www.nrlc.org/ ReaganProclamation.html*.

Some pro-choice advocates argue that, in earlier stages of development, the zygote, embryo, or fetus is not a fully formed human being and is therefore not a person. Pro-life advocates point out that many animals go through even more radical changes than humans. A frog begins its life outside the egg as a tadpole, and a butterfly was a caterpillar earlier in its life. In an article for *The New Oxford Review*, Eugene Hoyas wrote, "Most people understand that a frog never becomes an elephant. A frog is a frog. . . . But is a tadpole a frog . . . ? The tadpole has no lungs; it has gills. It has no legs; it has a tail. It looks and acts just like a fish."[47] Despite the differences in morphology (physical form) and physiology (functioning), Hoyas explained, "The biologist will not hesitate to affirm that the tadpole is indeed a frog."[48] The reason that the biologist categorizes a tadpole as a frog is that "the genetic code—the DNA blueprint that defines this particular organism—never changes. For this reason, no biologist ever confuses form with substance when establishing the identity of an organism."[49] Therefore, he asserted, an unborn child is a person at any stage of development.

> • **What is the difference between comparing a tadpole and a frog and comparing an embryo and a young child?**

Hoyas took the argument a step further, criticizing the pro-choice viewpoint that life does not begin until certain physical characteristics—such as a beating heart—are met. "That would be like saying the benchmark of life for the butterfly organism is the presence of wings and antennae and then, after examining the caterpillar, pronouncing that, because it has neither wings nor antennae, it is neither living nor a butterfly. . . ."[50]

In his article, Beckwith took pro-choice advocates to task for their assertions that the unborn child is not a person until it develops certain abilities. He noted that most developmental milestones, such as ability to think or feel, offered as the beginning of personhood are functional definitions, meaning that "if and only if an entity functions in a certain way are we warranted in calling that entity a person."[51] The problem with such functional assessments, he maintained, is that, even after birth, not all people meet these criteria, and yet the law considers them people. He wrote, "When a human being is asleep, unconscious, and temporarily comatose, she is not functioning as a person as defined by some personhood criteria. Nevertheless, most people would reject the notion that a human being is not a person while in any of these states."[52]

Pro-life advocates also point out that, outside of the context of abortion, people refer to unborn children as babies all the time. Keith Fournier and William Watkins of the American Center for Law and Justice (ACLJ) wrote, "When a woman miscarries and mourns the loss of her baby, she does not cry out, 'I lost the fetus . . . this lump of cells. . . .' No, she grieves over the death of her child, a real human person she has already grown to love and cherish. . . ."[53]

Perhaps it cannot be proved that personhood begins at conception, pro-life advocates say, but it also cannot be proved it does not. Pro-life writer Mary Meehan admonished the American Civil Liberties Union (ACLU) and other pro-choice supporters that, instead of assuming an unborn child is not a person, they should be "like the hunter who sees movement in the brush but does not know whether it is caused by a deer or another hunter. He must not shoot first and ask questions later. He has an obligation to find out whether a person is there; if so, or if he cannot find out, he has no right to shoot."[54]

Important rights are denied because of current legal standards.

Although many Americans strongly believe that life starts at conception, laws traditionally have not recognized the "personhood" of unborn children. Most significant, in the 1973 *Roe* v. *Wade* case, the U.S. Supreme Court ruled that women have a constitutional right to choose abortion in certain situations and that an unborn child is not a "person" protected by the

Fourteenth Amendment, which upholds the right to life, liberty, and property.

Pro-life advocates deny the existence of a "right to choose" and look forward to the eventual overturning of *Roe v. Wade*, arguing that the right to life is the most important right that an unborn child can have. *The Gift of Life* noted, "The human being is to be respected and treated as a person from the moment of conception; and therefore from that same moment his rights as a person must be recognized, among which in the first place is the inviolable right of every innocent human being to life." [55]

Pro-life advocates also note that abortion is not the only situation in which the rights of unborn children are at stake. Recognizing that the right to abortion is—for the time being, at least—protected by the Supreme Court's reading of the U.S. Constitution, many pro-life advocates have shifted their efforts to the many situations in which an unborn child's rights are implicated but the mother's choice and privacy are not issues. For example, when a pregnant women is attacked, hurt in a collision, or exposed to harmful chemicals and loses her unborn child as a result, many people, even many abortion rights supporters, believe that the unborn child should be protected by law. Some people would go farther, allowing the unborn to inherit property and receive social benefits. Immigration lawyers have even argued that a pregnant illegal immigrant should not be deported because her unborn child should be entitled to citizenship, just as a child born in the United States would be. Defense lawyers have argued that a pregnant woman cannot be imprisoned because the detention of her unborn child is unlawful.

Some pro-life advocates have compared *Roe v. Wade* to the Supreme Court's notorious decision in the *Dred Scott v. Sandford* case, which held that the Constitution was not intended to include slaves—or any other person of African ancestry—and therefore, African Americans were not entitled to any of the "rights and privileges" of citizens. [56] In a speech on the floor of the U.S. House of Representatives, Representative Mike Pence, an Indiana Republican, said:

> It is almost eerie at times how the parallels between the arguments of those 150 years ago advocating slavery rights match with the arguments of personal choice that support abortion today. . . .
>
> In the *Dred Scott* case, the Court stripped away all rights from a class of human beings and reduced them to nothing more than the property of others . . . and in *Roe* v. *Wade* the unborn child is simply considered the property of the mother in a legal sense.[57]

Pro-life advocates have made some inroads in changing laws to recognize the personhood of unborn children, and they believe that *Roe* v. *Wade* poses no legal barrier to doing so. Pro-choice advocates frequently cite the case to support the theory that a fetus is not a "person," legally speaking. Pro-life advocates quickly point out several problems. Among the problems cited are that the Court in *Roe* v. *Wade* did not take a position as to when life begins and that subsequent decisions open the door for defining personhood as beginning at conception.

• Do you think comparisons between *Dred Scott* and *Roe* v. *Wade* are valid?

In *Roe* v. *Wade*, the Court did not specifically find that life begins at birth. Rather, it ruled that there was no historical indication that in 1868 the writers of the Fourteenth Amendment, which prohibits states from "depriv[ing] any person of life, liberty, or property,"[58] intended to include unborn children within its definition of a "person."[59]

Pro-life advocates have criticized the Court's avoidance of the issue, saying that, by not taking a position on the issue of when life begins, the Court has allowed the rights of the unborn to be trampled. Francis Beckwith accused the Court of hypocrisy when he wrote, "Although verbally the Court denied taking sides, [it effectively ruled] that the fetus is not a human person worthy of protection in this society."[60] In fact, the Supreme Court ruled ten years after *Roe* v. *Wade* that "a State may not adopt one theory of when life begins to justify its regulation of abortions."[61]

The Court's neutrality on the question appears to be shifting toward the acceptance of the personhood of the unborn. In the 1989 *Webster* v. *Reproductive Health Services* case, the Court upheld a law enacted by the state of Missouri that declares, "The life of each human being begins at conception," and thus "unborn children have protectable interests in life, health, and well-being."[62] Although pro-choice advocates denounced the *Webster* decision, this part of the ruling did not have an impact on abortion rights because the law in question specifically mentioned that the rights of the unborn were limited by the U.S. Supreme Court's rulings on abortion rights.

The legal system has begun to recognize the personhood of unborn children.

The *Webster* case's treatment of personhood, while not having much of an impact on abortion rights, has inspired a number of laws at both the state and federal level that recognize the personhood of an unborn child. Many of these laws came about after state court decisions ruled that unborn children are not "people." Courts based these decisions on "common law" principles, in which the interpretation of laws is based on the previous decisions of judges and modified from time to time by other judges as circumstances change. The reason that courts issue written opinions in many cases is so that these opinions can serve as the basis for future decisions.

Pro-choice advocates often point out that the tradition of the common law does not support recognition of fetuses as "people." Common law embraced the "born-alive rule," which held that a child must have been born alive to have legal standing as a person. Pro-life advocates are quick to respond that, although common law provides guidance to courts in interpreting laws, the U.S. Congress and the individual state legislatures are free to make decisions that reject common law traditions, and in fact, many states and the U.S. Congress have recognized that an unborn child can be considered a person.

A 2001 ruling by the Supreme Court of Arkansas provides an excellent example of how decisions by legislatures can have an impact on the way that courts apply common law traditions. Traditionally, parents could not sue for the wrongful death of an unborn child, and as recently as 1995, the same court, following the common law "born-alive rule," had ruled that parents could not bring lawful death suits that involved children who were not born alive. In the 2001 *Aka* v. *Jefferson Hospital Association* case, however, the court relied on several state laws to reverse its 1995 decision. For example, the state constitution declares, "The policy of Arkansas is to protect the life of every unborn child from conception until birth, to the extent permitted by the Federal Constitution."[63] In addition, the state's homicide laws note that the term *person* "includes an unborn child in utero at any stage of development.... 'Unborn child' means a living fetus of twelve (12) weeks or greater gestation."[64]

> • **How should judges decide when it is right to depart from legal tradition?**

As a result of actions by the state legislature, the *Aka* court ruled that a constitutional amendment and several state laws had nullified the common law restrictions and that the Akas could sue the doctors and hospital for wrongful death after the stillbirth of their child. The court wrote:

> Given this amended definition of "person," the legislature plainly affords protection to unborn viable fetuses, assuming injury or death occurred without the mother's consent to a lawful abortion or outside the "usual and customary standards of medical practice" or beyond "acts deemed

necessary to save" the mother's life. The relevance of the legislature's response, by statutorily defining person in the criminal context to include a fetus, cannot be understated given our strong reliance in [the 1995 case, which] was predicated upon the lack of legislative guidance in defining the term "person." As a result, this court was obliged to turn to the common-law definition of person, which did not include a viable fetus . . . . [If] there had been any doubt concerning the State's public policy on this subject, it is now laid to rest. We are no longer constrained by the common-law definition of person.[65]

A number of other states have passed laws similar to those of Arkansas, and, at the federal level, several laws in recent years have addressed the personhood of unborn children. In 2002, the Bush administration announced that SCHIP, which gives federal funding to states in order to provide health care to children from low-income families, could also receive federal funding to provide prenatal care to pregnant women. Although the program is designed specifically to benefit children, the administration justified its expansion of the program by declaring, "Child means an individual under the age of 19 including the period from conception to birth."[66] Pro-life advocates hailed this regulation as a positive step toward the legal recognition of unborn children as people, but it was a policy of the Bush administration, which carries less weight than an act of Congress.

Congress followed suit in 2004 with the passage of the Unborn Victims of Violence Act, which is discussed in detail in later chapters. The law, under which a person can be charged with murder for ending a woman's pregnancy through a violent assault or the mother's murder, states that "a member of the species homo sapiens, at any stage of development, who is carried in the womb" is to be considered an "unborn child."[67] Although the law itself applies in limited circumstances, pro-life advocates are hopeful that the definition of "unborn child" will influence courts to grant personhood to unborn children under other circumstances.

Compromise solutions such as setting viability as the start of life are unworkable.

Some pro-choice advocates have taken a position that, if the beginning of personhood is not set at birth, it should at least be set at some time later than conception. John Walker of Libertarians for Life charges that, by seeking a time other than conception for the beginning of personhood, pro-choice advocates "have assumed that [the beginning of personhood] happens at some time convenient enough to permit abortions, and then set out to prove this time or that."[68] In his opinion, pro-choice advocates seek to establish the "fact" of the beginning of personhood in order to support their conclusion that abortion should be legal rather than basing their conclusion on known facts.

A common suggestion for the start of personhood is viability. In the regulation of abortion, the Supreme Court has held that states have great leeway in regulating abortions after the point of viability, the point at which the unborn child can live outside the womb. Although many pro-choice advocates believe that the privileges and rights of personhood should be given only after birth, some have suggested viability as a compromise position. The reasoning is that such a definition would not have a major impact on abortion rights, because postviability abortions are already heavily regulated.

Pro-life advocates reject this compromise on moral grounds. Dissenting in the 1989 *Webster* case, Chief Justice William Rehnquist, joined by several other conservative justices, wrote, "We do not see why the State's interest in protecting potential human life should come into existence only at the point of viability, and that there should therefore be a rigid line allowing state regulation [of abortion] after viability but prohibiting it before viability."[69]

• **Is there a difference in the value of the life of a viable fetus and a nonviable fetus?**

Another criticism is that viability is a "moving target," with medical science making the point of viability increasingly early. In the *Webster* case, the Knights of Columbus, a national Catholic men's organization argued:

> Viability is an invalid benchmark for construing the meaning of "person" in the Fourteenth Amendment because it has nothing to do with attributes of personhood, or a particularized state of being, but only the state of medical technology. Viability's true utility lies in its insight that a viable infant is certainly a person and that only limitations on technology prevent all unborn children from being viable. If a viable unborn child is a person, then so are all unborn children, viable or not. . . .[70]

In a 2004 case, a justice of the Supreme Court of Kentucky, dissenting from the court's reading of a criminal statute, optimistically predicted, "The advances of medical science are limitless and can be easily applied to enlarge the viability concept to currently unknown dimensions, including fertilization and conception."[71]

Summary

Many pro-life advocates argue that new technology that allows physicians and scientists to trace prenatal development demonstrates that an unborn child is a person from the moment of conception onward and therefore deserves the same legal rights as everyone else. They note that many jurisdictions are beginning to recognize the obsolescence of the traditional legal view that an unborn child is not a person.

Fetal Homicide Laws Threaten Women's Rights

Testifying before Congress in 2003, Juley Fulcher, an attorney who represented victims of domestic violence and the public policy director of the National Coalition Against Domestic Violence, told a heart-wrenching story:

> Several years ago, a client of mine lost a pregnancy due to domestic violence. There was a history of domestic violence in her case and she had sought assistance several times. While she was 8 months pregnant, her batterer lifted her up in his arms and held her body horizontal to the ground. He then slammed her body to the floor causing her to miscarry. . . . It was clear by the batterer's words and actions that his intent was to cause physical and emotional injury to the woman and establish undeniably his power to control her.[72]

Fulcher was testifying in opposition to UVVA, which was signed into law the following year by President George W. Bush and declared that an attack on an embryo or fetus can be charged as an assault or homicide in federal criminal prosecutions. Fulcher and many other feminists oppose such laws because they consider women the true victims of such crimes.

Feminists continue to oppose efforts to pass laws like UVVA at the state level. Under most circumstances, federal laws trump state laws. For example, when federal pollution standards are stricter than state pollution standards, manufacturers have to follow federal law. Criminal law is different. Following legal tradition, most crimes are prosecuted by the states. The states have general "police power," meaning that they can enforce whatever laws the people of the state enact, unless the U.S. Constitution specifically prohibits that type of law. In contrast, the U.S. Constitution limits the power of the federal government to those "enumerated powers" that are specifically listed in the Constitution. The federal government enforces a number of criminal laws related to those powers. For example, it makes robbing a post office a federal offense because the federal government has the power to maintain a post office. The most significant power that justifies federal criminal laws is Congress's power to regulate interstate commerce. Therefore, Congress can pass laws that criminalize acts such as hijacking an airplane.

Federal prosecutions for murder are generally limited to special circumstances, such as when the murder is committed in connection with another federal crime or when the murder takes place in a federal jurisdiction such as a national park, military facility, or Washington, D.C. Even now that UVVA has become federal law, most murders will be prosecuted under state law and people will be charged with fetal homicide only in states that recognize such laws. At the time of UVVA's passage, more than half of U.S. states had laws that recognized fetal homicide as a crime, but several state legislatures have taken up the issue since then. Fulcher and other women's rights advocates want a solution to the problem of violence against pregnant women, but they do not like the approach taken by UVVA and state fetal homicide laws.

> • **Should Congress have the power to enact criminal laws that apply to all cases, regardless of the circumstances?**

Fetal homicide laws do not address the underlying problem of violence against women.

Committing a violent act against an embryo or fetus, as envisioned by UVVA and similar state laws, is impossible without simultaneously committing a violent act against a woman. For years, women's groups have been pushing for stronger laws to punish violence against women, with mixed results. Although the number of reported incidences of violence against women has gone down, many crimes go unreported or unpunished. Pro-life advocates were able to persuade Congress to act with great ceremony and publicity to punish the much smaller number of cases in which an embryo or fetus is harmed.

The federal Bureau of Justice Statistics noted that, in 2001, nearly 700,000 reported violent crimes were committed against "intimate partners" by spouses, former spouses, boyfriends, and girlfriends.[73] The report also concluded that intimate partners committed 20 percent of nonfatal violent acts against women, including rape, sexual assault, robbery, aggravated assault, and simple assault. Intimate partners also murdered 1,247 women in 2000. In fact, in recent years, intimate partners have committed about one out of every three murders of women.

Another report placed the number of nonfatal violent crimes much higher, estimating that "approximately 4.9 million intimate partner rapes and physical assaults are perpetrated against U.S. women annually."[74] The reason for the much higher figures is that many women are either afraid of further violence or believe that the police will not help. The report found:

Most intimate partner victimizations are not reported to the police. Only approximately one-fifth of all rapes, one-quarter of all physical assaults, and one-half of all stalkings perpetrated against female respondents by intimates were reported to the police. . . . The majority of victims who did not report their victimization to the police thought the police would not or could not do anything on their behalf. These findings suggest that most victims of intimate partner violence do not consider the justice system an appropriate vehicle for resolving conflicts with intimates.[75]

THE LETTER OF THE LAW

When Does Killing an Embryo or Fetus Become Criminal Homicide?

Federal law recognizes killing an embryo or fetus (except by medical abortion) as murder, from conception onward. Most crimes are prosecuted under state law, however, and many states recognize only embryos or fetuses at later stages of development as murder victims.

At conception: Utah homicide laws include killing "an unborn child at any stage of its development." Utah Code Sec. 76-5-201.

At the end of the embryonic stage: California defines murder as the "unlawful killing of a human being, or a fetus," but the law does not include embryos. Cal. Penal Code Sec. 187(a).

At 12 weeks: Arkansas criminalizes the killing of an "unborn child," defined as "a living fetus of twelve (12) weeks or greater gestation." Ark. Code Sec. 5-1-102(13)(B).

At quickening: Florida law considers "willful killing of an unborn quick child" to be manslaughter, if it results from a violent act that would have been considered murder if the mother had died. Fla. Stat. Section 782.09.

At viability: Tennessee homicide laws include in their definition of "person" the "viable fetus of a human being." Tenn. Code Section 39-13-214.

When the Judiciary Committee of the U.S. House of Representatives issued its report on UVVA, several representatives disagreed with the report's conclusion and issued their own dissenting views. One of their primary concerns was the law's failure to address the tremendous problem of violence against women. They wrote, "[UVVA] vests rights in the fetus, but does not respond to violence against women, and fails to recognize that an injury to a fetus is first and foremost an injury to the woman, and, in the case of a live birth, an injury to that individual."[76] The dissenting representatives explained that UVVA, like current federal laws, "[fails] to address the vast number of domestic violence acts perpetrated against women and prosecuted under State statutes. UVVA and other Federal statutes currently on the books directed at interstate domestic violence, stalking and violations of protection orders would have no effect on these cases."[77]

Although they did not deny that attacks on women that lead to miscarriage or stillbirth of an embryo or fetus are serious problems in need of a federal response, the dissenting representatives accused the bill's sponsors of being more concerned with the welfare of the embryo or fetus than the welfare of the women who carried them. They argued:

> If the sponsors were legitimately concerned with the problem of violence against women, they should focus their efforts on the real problem of violence against pregnant women and full funding of the Violence Against Women Act, which expanded protections for women against acts of violence regardless of their pregnancy status. Tellingly, in fiscal year 2003, Congress appropriated $107,200,000 less than the fully authorized level. Programs including transitional housing, Federal victims counselors, and training for judges were not funded at all. Rape prevention/education was appropriated at half its authorized level.[78]

"Single-victim" laws are an effective alternative to fetal homicide laws.

The dissenting representatives proposed an alternative solution to the serious problem of violence against pregnant women. Their alternate solution reflected their view that attacks on an embryo or fetus are inherently attacks against women. By reclassifying the murder of a pregnant woman—at any time after conception—as two separate murders with two equal victims, the dissenters noted, "the sponsors intend to equate the rights of a zygote with those of a fully mature woman whose constitutional rights have vested at birth."[79]

Instead, the dissenters supported an alternative version of the bill proposed by California Democrat Zoe Lofgren. The "Motherhood Protection Act" proposed by Lofgren called for vastly increased penalties for anyone who violates a federal law and thereby "causes an interruption to the normal course of the pregnancy that results in prenatal injury (including termination of the pregnancy)."[80] Under Lofgren's proposal, the penalties would be severe and the law would recognize two separate crimes but only a "single victim," the woman against whom the violence was committed. In support of her amendment, Lofgren argued that the bill was necessary to recognize the harm caused to the woman by the violent termination of a pregnancy: "[When] crimes hurt a pregnant woman and cause her to miscarry there is an additional and very serious harm to that woman. This amendment creates a second separate offense with severe and consistent penalties for causing this additional harm, up to a life sentence."[81]

Lofgren noted that, in part, she based her desire to punish "fetal homicide" as a crime against the woman rather than a crime against the fetus on her own life experience. She stated:

> [The] absolute most exciting moment of my entire life
> was when I gave birth to my children. . . . And for anyone
> who has had a miscarriage, as I have had, you know the

disappointment, really the devastation that comes with that loss. There is nothing really larger than to lose a pregnancy and to not have the child that you thought you would have. It is something that you really never get over. But when that is something that really comes from the hand of God rather than the hand of an assault, you make your peace with it. To imagine that that loss would be caused by the violence of another is really unbelievable and really deserves the very largest penalty that we can possibly devise, because to deny a woman the opportunity to have her much desired child is a lifelong sentence. And those who would assault someone and cause a miscarriage, they deserve a life sentence, in my judgment, for the harm that they have done.[82]

Despite the harsh penalties proposed by Lofgren's bill, pro-life advocates lobbied heavily against it and the final language of UVVA recognizes two victims, treating the woman and the embryo or fetus as two separate individuals.

> • **Does it make sense to say that a person can commit two murders with only one victim? Is this a fair characterization of single-victim laws?**

The true purpose of fetal homicide laws is to undermine abortion rights.

Although women's rights activists were concerned that UVVA did not take crimes against women seriously, their bigger concern was that the law's true purpose was not to protect embryos and fetuses from violent assaults against women but instead to set the groundwork for overruling *Roe* v. *Wade* and its guarantee of abortion rights. A key holding of *Roe* v. *Wade* is that an embryo or a fetus is not a "person" entitled to protection under the U.S. Constitution because laws traditionally had not recognized an embryo or fetus as a person. One way for pro-life advocates to undermine the right to abortion is to lobby for laws that do

Charges could double for fetal homicide

There are 30 states that treat the unlawful killing of an unborn child as a homicide. State laws differ, especially on how many weeks old a fetus must be to become a homicide victim.

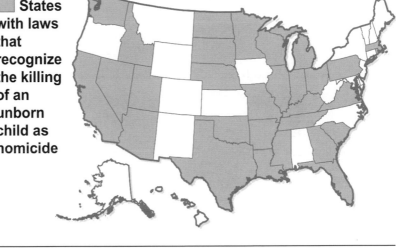

States with laws that recognize the killing of an unborn child as homicide

SOURCE: National Right to Life   AP

Thirty states allow the unlawful killing of an unborn child to be classified as a homicide. Many pro-choice advocates fear that these laws will eventually lead to overturning *Roe* v. *Wade*. Most pro-life advocates, by contrast, believe that a fetus, or unborn child, should have all the same rights as any human being.

recognize an embryo or fetus as a person, thereby slowly changing legal traditions and influencing future cases that interpret the Constitution.

By referring to "a child, who is in utero"—defined as "a member of the species homo sapiens, at any stage of development, who is carried in the womb"[83]—the law recognizes an embryo or fetus as a "child," and a child is clearly a person. An embryo or fetus is clearly a person under this law. For the first time, pro-life advocates succeeded in passing a federal law that recognizes an embryo or fetus as a person. Abortion rights supporters tried in vain to stop the federal law. While the House of Representatives was deliberating on UVVA, NARAL issued the following statement:

> Congress could easily pass a bill that would punish criminals and honor families' losses without entangling the issue in the abortion rights debate at all. But the anti-choice leadership of the U.S. House of Representatives hopes to chip away at women's rights by passing this deceitful legislation. In Tom DeLay's House, protecting families and punishing criminals is less important than taking advantage of tragedy to promote the far-right agenda of trying to rob women of their right to choose.[84]

Lofgren argued that her "single-victim" bill could accomplish law enforcement goals without jeopardizing abortion rights:

> [We should not use violence against pregnant women] as an excuse to cut away at the right of American women to make their own personal choices about reproduction. Although the proponents of the bill argue that it has nothing to do with abortion, in fact it does. Senator Orrin Hatch, the Chairman of the Senate Judiciary Committee, admitted on their side of the building in the other body that the measure would have an impact on abortion law. And he said this, quote: They say it undermines abortion rights. It does undermine it, he said, but that is irrelevant. We are concerned here about a woman and her child. The partisan arguments over abortion should not stop a bill that protects women and children.[85]

Law professor Michael Dorf suggested that another alternative would be to follow the example of states that have criminalized feticide but do not define the embryo or fetus as a person. In his column for *FindLaw's Writ,* he noted, "California's law is illustrative. It defines murder as the killing of a human being *or* a fetus."[86] The law recognizes the embryo or fetus as a second victim, but it does not cloud abortion rights by extending the definition of personhood to an embryo or fetus.

Lofgren's "single-victim" bill was rejected, and Congress passed UVVA by a wide margin with language that recognizes an embryo or fetus as an unborn child who can be a distinct victim of crime. After President Bush signed the bill into law, Kim Gandy, president of NOW, commented, "George W. Bush and his anti-abortion allies are gloating today because they have exploited the devastating murder of a woman to attack the reproductive rights of all women."[87]

Pro-choice advocates have not given up the battle. Now that UVVA has passed at the federal level and many states have enacted similar laws, they are attempting to develop legal theories to explain how abortion might remain a constitutional right even though the laws recognize an embryo or fetus as a person. In the original *Roe* v. *Wade* ruling, the Supreme Court held that "by adopting one theory of life, Texas may [not] override the rights of the pregnant woman that are at stake."[88] Today, pro-choice advocates are trying to prevent the rights given to embryos and fetuses by certain laws from overriding abortion rights.

Michael Dorf has argued that establishing the personhood of an embryo or fetus in one context—defining who can be the victim of murder or assault—does not necessarily establish the personhood of an embryo or fetus in the context of abortion law. He pointed out that courts have long ruled that corporations "are 'persons' under the Fourteenth Amendment in the sense that their property cannot be taken without fair processes, but not in the sense that they are entitled to vote on equal terms with natural persons." [89] He interpreted *Roe* v. *Wade* to require "that in a conflict with the constitutional liberty of a pregnant woman seeking an abortion before [viability], the fetus may not be given the same rights as the woman." [90]

> • **Do you believe that the real purpose of fetal homicide laws is to topple abortion rights?**

The chief justice of Utah's Supreme Court argued a similar position in a 2004 dissenting opinion. The state of Utah had passed a fetal homicide law that defines homicide as "[causing]

FROM THE BENCH

Utah's Chief Justice: Fetal Homicide Laws Conflict With Abortion Rights.

In 2004, Utah's Supreme Court held that the murder of a pregnant woman resulted in the murder of two "people." Chief Justice Christine Durham dissented. She argued that the state of Utah did not have the power to declare an embryo or a fetus a person because doing so conflicted with the federal constitutional right to choose an abortion.

Preliminarily, it is clear that the legislature is entitled to protect to the fullest extent pregnant mothers and their expectations of bringing their pregnancies to term. Even supporters of legal abortion agree that an assault [that] destroys a developing fetus is a particularly heinous crime.... A violent attack by a third person on a mother that also kills her fetus injures more than the mother alone. One of the most fundamental of life's experiences has been cut short; parents' aspirations to bring forth a new generation have been shattered; a family that could have been will not be; a life that could have developed into an independent individual has been extinguished. We need not enter into any debate regarding the status of the fetus itself to see that a state may freely increase penalties for a homicide or an assault that also kills a fetus: respect for the mother alone would be sufficient. The power of the legislature to classify a homicide that also unlawfully destroys a fetus as aggravated murder, then, is not at issue here. The problem is, rather, that the legislature has not clearly done so.

the death of another human being, including an unborn child."[91] The defendant in the case, who had been accused of killing a pregnant woman, was charged with "aggravated homicide," a more serious offense. A defendant can be charged with aggravated homicide in Utah if "two or more persons were killed."[92] Although the state's highest court refused to dismiss the charges, its chief justice disagreed, arguing that defining a "human being" to include an "unborn child" in one law did not necessarily mean that an "unborn child" was a "person" for the purposes of another law.

The aggravated homicide statute applies when two "persons" are killed, and a fetus is not a person under our law.

"Person" is a legal category with important consequences. Most important, persons are entitled to rights under the Fourteenth Amendment of the United States Constitution. It would be an obvious denial of equal protection to allow doctors, or anyone else, to kill one "person" in order to save another, and clearly a denial of due process to permit this without any legal process at all. Thus, declaring a fetus to be a "person" entitled to equal protection would require not only overturning *Roe* v. *Wade*, 410 U.S. 113 (1973), but also making abortion, as a matter of constitutional law, illegal in all circumstances, even to save the life of the mother....

To declare a fetus a "person" is beyond the power of the state of Utah, whether acting through either its legislature or its courts. A state cannot overrule the United States Supreme Court by changing who counts as a "person" for constitutional purposes.

Finally, even if the Utah Legislature could define "person" to include a fetus, which I believe it cannot, the legislature does not seem to have done so. At any rate, no statutory language defining "person," as opposed to "unborn child" or "human being" has been cited to us.

Source: *State* v. *MacGuire*, 84 P.3d 1171 (Utah 2004) (Durham, C.J., dissenting).

Chief Justice Christine Durham based her argument on two main points. Her first point was that the Utah legislature had not explicitly defined "person" to include an embryo or fetus. Her second point was that, if the legislature had explicitly defined an embryo or fetus to be a "person," the law would have been unconstitutional. According to her logic, recognition of the embryo or fetus as a person would require "making abortion, as a matter of constitutional law, illegal in all circumstances, even to save the life of the mother," [93] because the Fourteenth Amendment to the U.S. Constitution requires states to protect a person's life. The current state of constitutional law holds that states cannot ban all abortions. Therefore, she reasoned, the only way for the state to protect the life of every person constitutionally is to use a definition of "person" that excludes embryos and fetuses.

Law professor Alec Walen has proposed that, even if an embryo or a fetus is determined to be a "person" whose life must be protected by the state, abortion could nevertheless remain legal. Essentially, he reframed the act of abortion from killing to refusing to provide life support. Walen wrote that, if the embryo or fetus had the legal status of a person, then "it might seem that it would be permissible to kill [the embryo or fetus] only if necessary to save the mother's life or to protect her from grievous bodily harm"—the circumstances under which killing another person in self-defense is justified.[94] He questioned whether, regardless of legal status, an embryo or fetus would necessarily have the right to "life support" from a pregnant woman. He pointed out that a parent cannot be compelled by law to donate a kidney, or even a pint of blood, to a living child, and he concluded, "The duty to serve as life support for another is altogether different from the duty not to kill another who is living on his or her own."[95] Therefore, even if a state had the constitutional duty to protect the lives of embryos and fetuses, it would not have to require a woman to carry a pregnancy to term—except for viable fetuses, who can live without a woman's "life support."

- **Does recognition of an unborn child as a person in one law mean that the definition of "person" in all laws includes unborn children?**

Covering embryos and nonviable fetuses raises too many questions.

Viability is an important benchmark in abortion law, and some have suggested that it should be a benchmark in fetal homicide laws. States place fewer restrictions on abortion before viability; however, this distinction is based on Supreme Court rulings that, after viability, the state's interest in protecting life outweighs a woman's right to privacy. Although no Supreme Court ruling guides states in crafting fetal homicide laws, some states have chosen to protect only viable fetuses under fetal homicide laws. Other states have chosen a point—such as quickening (when the baby first moves) or the twelfth week of pregnancy—well after UVVA, which covers an embryo or fetus "at any stage of development, who is carried in the womb."[96]

Arguments in favor of including only fetuses at later stages of development are likely motivated by concerns about abortion rights: Pro-choice advocates fear that fetal homicide laws will erode abortion rights, but postviability abortions are already highly restricted. Opponents of fetal homicide law also raise practical questions about how the homicide of an embryo or fetus can be proven "beyond a reasonable doubt," as is required for criminal convictions.

During deliberations over UVVA, Representative Carolyn Maloney of New York blasted UVVA for "criminaliz[ing] actions that can occur at the very earliest phases of pregnancy," noting, "roughly 20 to 25 percent of all pregnancies end in miscarriage."[97] Obstetricians sometimes advise their patients not to announce pregnancy too widely until the second trimester or until an ultrasound detects a heartbeat because of the high number of miscarriages that occur before these events. Maloney suggested that law enforcement officials would have difficulty determining whether the miscarriage resulted from a violent act or another cause. "Usually there is a genetic reason [for a miscarriage], but sometimes there is another cause. Studies show that miscarriages can occur because of excessive coffee drinking, smoking, exposure to chemicals, illness, stress or trauma during an accident," she said.[98]

> • Because UVVA limits fetal homicide charges to cases in which another federal law is broken, is there any chance that the law will be used to prosecute people who serve coffee to pregnant women?

She expressed concern that a number of "relatively innocent actions" could trigger a miscarriage early in pregnancy, leading to unexpected murder charges for someone who would have no way of knowing that a woman was pregnant. She asked:

> If someone comes to work, for example, with German measles, knowing that they could infect a fellow worker, could they be guilty of manslaughter? Will Starbucks have to post signs advising pregnant women that they cannot buy more than two cups of coffee per day? Will car manufacturers face imprisonment for miscarriages caused by steering wheels, seat belts or air bags? Will airlines face criminal charges if they permit pregnant women to fly? Will bodega owners be charged for selling pregnant women cigarettes?[99]

Summary

Feminists and pro-choice activists want something done to stop violence against women, especially pregnant women. They maintain, however, that an assault or murder that leads to a miscarriage or stillbirth should be prosecuted as a serious crime against a woman, not as two separate crimes. Defining an embryo or fetus as a potential murder victim, they fear, could be used as a stepping stone toward outlawing abortion.

Laws Must Protect Every Unborn Child From Violence

In 1992, five days before their son was due, Tracy Marciniak's husband attacked her brutally in their Milwaukee home. She recalls in chilling detail how her husband's obvious purpose was to kill their unborn son, whom Tracy had planned to name Zachariah:

> He held me against a couch by my hair. He knew that I very much wanted my son. He punched me very hard twice in the abdomen. Then he refused to call for help, and prevented me from calling.
>
> After about 15 minutes of my screaming in pain that I needed help, he finally went to a bar and from there called for help. I and Zachariah were rushed by ambulance to the hospital, where Zachariah was delivered by emergency Caesarean section. My son was dead. The physicians

said he had bled to death inside me because of blunt-force trauma.[100]

While Tracy was spending three weeks in the hospital recovering from life-threatening injuries, she received some news that made her emotional pain even worse: Law enforcement officials had visited her sister and told her that, under Wisconsin law, they could not charge Tracy's husband with murder. Tracy recalls:

> [When] I was told that in the eyes of the law, no murder had occurred[,] I was devastated. My life already seemed destroyed by the loss of my son. But there was so much additional pain because the law was blind to what had really happened. The law, which I had been raised to believe was based on justice, was telling me that Zachariah had not really been murdered.[101]

Although prosecutors tried to charge Tracy's husband with violating a 1955 abortion law, they were not able to convict him for any crime against Zachariah, only for his attack on Tracy. Despite his deliberate actions in punching Tracy in the abdomen, Wisconsin law did not recognize his act as murder.

Tracy took some solace in 1998, when Governor Tommy Thompson signed a law that recognizes what Tracy's husband had done as an act of murder. At least Tracy knew that other Wisconsin women and their families would not have to suffer through learning that the law did not recognize the deaths of their unborn children crimes. Tracy went to Capitol Hill in 2003 to urge Congress to pass a similar law at the federal level. Because most murders are prosecuted under state law, advocates will continue to push for laws in the more than 20 states that did not have fetal homicide laws at the time that UVVA was passed.

- **In the case of a violent attack that leads to miscarriage, would a single-victim law be an adequate substitute? Could the surviving woman be considered a murder victim?**

Unborn victim laws are needed to punish horrible crimes.

A major criticism of unborn victim laws has been that the laws do not address the problem of violence against women. Although the laws do define the unborn child, rather than the mother, as the victim, they provide for serious punishment of the offender. Senator Orrin Hatch of Utah rejects claims that unborn victim laws ignore the problem of violence against women. Rather, he classified unborn victim laws as part of an overall campaign to fight domestic violence. In a speech on the Senate floor, he said:

> I believe domestic violence is an evil plague that needs to be stopped. . . . My commitment to this issue has been long-standing. As many of my colleagues are aware, I was an original cosponsor of the Violence Against Women Act over a decade ago, and I have tirelessly fought in countless venues to protect the rights of women. This bill furthers that cause.
>
> For many years, I have worked hard on the issue of domestic violence and violence against women, and when I stand here today before the entire Senate and offer my support for a bill, I certainly make sure that bill does not diminish in any way our capacity to curb domestic violence and protect women.[102]

In fact, Hatch argued, unborn victim laws help fight domestic violence by defining fetal homicide as a serious crime. He noted that UVVA "empowers abused women because it gives the Government a greater arsenal of prosecutorial tools to put the abusive spouse behind bars for a longer period of time."[103]

"Single-victim" laws are inadequate.

Pro-choice advocates have generally opposed unborn victim laws because they fear that recognizing that an unborn child can be a victim of a homicide would threaten abortion rights. Some laws, such as California's fetal homicide statute, explicitly differentiate between a "person" and an unborn child—the California law refers to the "unlawful killing of a human being, or a fetus." At the federal level, California Representative Zoe Lofgren, a Democrat, proposed the "Motherhood Protection Act" as an alternative to UVVA. This law would recognize a "single victim" when an unborn child is killed—the pregnant woman. Pro-choice advocates argued that single-victim laws adequately address the violent crime of killing or harming an unborn child.

> • **Are laws that outlaw the killing of a "fetus" an adequate substitute for laws that recognize unborn children as murder victims on equal footing with people already born?**

Supporters of unborn victim laws have a number of answers to advocates of single-victim laws; they say that single-victim laws are not adequate to address the horrible crimes addressed by unborn victim laws. Notre Dame law Professor Gerard Bradley testified in hearings on UVVA that the Motherhood Protection Act, with its increased penalties for an attack on a pregnant woman if her unborn child is harmed, was structurally very different from other criminal laws. He noted:

> The criminal law does not generally treat crimes against children as aggravations of an accompanying crime against a parent. (Think of the case where a single violent act, such as planting a bomb or starting a fire, kills an entire family.) For each victim, a distinct count, complete unto itself, for the injury or death of that particular individual is the norm.[104]

Opponents of single-victim laws deny that the elevated grief experienced by a pregnant woman justifies classifying a violent act as a single, more serious crime against the woman. Bradley noted, "I surely agree with the central notion of the [Motherhood Protection Act] (a notion entirely consistent with UVVA), that a mother suffers grievously with the injury or death of her child. This loss is particularly acute where the child is killed by a criminal act." [105] Bradley pointed out, however, that the reason behind this grief is that the mother has lost a child. He argued:

> [Suppose] a woman carries a child in utero, and does not seek an abortion. For all the world can see, she considers that child her baby, to be treated as such by everyone: her doctors, her family, the law. Upon that child's death she suffers, too, of course, but does she suffer more, or differently, than the woman who loses a newborn to a crime? A toddler? Who is to say? Is there any general answer? [106]

Although there might not be any way of comparing the grief of a mother who has lost an unborn child to one who has lost a newborn or toddler, the testimony of women who have lost unborn children in violent attacks shows that the grief is quite severe. Several women came forward to say that a single-victim law would not adequately address that grief. Tracy Marciniak brought with her a photograph in which she was holding her stillborn son at his funeral. She asked the members of the committee, "Does [this photograph] show one victim, or two?" and pleaded, "If you look at this photo and see two victims—a dead baby and a grieving mother who survived a brutal assault—then you should support the Unborn Victims of Violence Act." [107] Marciniak explained how a single-victim law would cause more even more grief to women who had lost their babies by denying that a murder took place:

> Some lawmakers say that criminals who attack pregnant women should be punished more severely, but that the law must never recognize someone's unborn child as a legal victim. For example, I have read Congresswoman Lofgren's proposal, which she calls the "Motherhood Protection Act." There is only one victim in that bill—the pregnant woman. So if you

vote for that bill, you are really saying all over again to me, "We're sorry, but nobody really died that night. There is no dead baby in the picture. You were the only victim." [108]

Serrin Foster, president of Feminists for Life of America, pointed out in her testimony that, when a pregnant woman is murdered, the surviving family should be allowed to grieve for two deaths, not one. Arguing against a single-victim law, Foster recounted the tragic story of a pregnant woman killed in the 1995 Oklahoma City bombing:

> After years of trying to have a child, Carrie and Michael Lenz, Jr., were overjoyed to learn that she was carrying their son, whom they named Michael Lenz III. Carrying a copy of the sonogram, Carrie went to work early the next morning to show coworkers the first photo of baby Michael. She and Michael were killed, along with three other pregnant women and their unborn children, when the Alfred P. Murrah Federal Building exploded on April 19, 1995. This father's agony was multiplied later when he saw that the memorial named only his wife, not his son, as a victim. In the eyes of the federal government, there was no second victim. Timothy McVeigh was never held accountable for killing Michael Lenz's namesake. [109]

In a letter to Massachusetts Senator John Kerry during his presidential campaign, Sharon Rocha, the mother of Laci Peterson, expressed similar sentiments as she urged him to support UVVA rather than the Motherhood Protection Act. Rocha pointed out that a single-victim law effectively would have denied Conner's existence. She wrote:

> Please understand how adoption of such a single-victim proposal would be a painful blow to those, like me, who are left to grieve after a two-victim crime, because Congress

would be saying that Conner and other innocent victims like
him are not really victims—indeed, that they never really
existed at all. But our grandson did live. He had a name, he
was loved, and his life was violently taken from him before he
ever saw the sun.[110]

THE LETTER OF THE LAW

The Unborn Victims of Violence Act, or "Laci and Conner's Law"

Under federal law, the murder of an unborn child, from conception on, is treated on par with the murder of a living person. Most crimes, however, are prosecuted under state law, and many states do not recognize killing an unborn child as murder. Other states' laws cover unborn children at later stages of development.

(a) (1) Whoever engages in conduct that violates [a federal law] and thereby causes the death of, or bodily injury . . . to, a child, who is in utero at the time the conduct takes place, is guilty of a separate offense under this section.

(2) (A) Except as otherwise provided in this paragraph, the punishment for that separate offense is the same as the punishment provided under Federal law for that conduct had that injury or death occurred to the unborn child's mother.

(B) An offense under this section does not require proof that—

(i) the person engaging in the conduct had knowledge or should have had knowledge that the victim of the underlying offense was pregnant; or

(ii) the defendant intended to cause the death of, or bodily injury to, the unborn child. . . .

(d) As used in this section, the term "unborn child" means a child in utero, and the term "child in utero" or "child, who is in utero" means a member of the species homo sapiens, at any stage of development, who is carried in the womb.

Source: Unborn Victims of Violence Act, Public Law No. 108-212, 108th Congress (2004).

- **Do you believe that single-victim laws are insensitive to crime victims and their families?**

When President Bush signed UVVA after its passage by Congress, he cited the testimony of Rocha and Marciniak as proof that single-victim laws do not serve justice or address a family's grief. He said:

> The death of an innocent unborn child has too often been treated as a detail in one crime, but not a crime in itself. Police and prosecutors had been to crime scenes and have shared the grief of families, but have so often been unable to seek justice for the full offense. The American people, as well, have learned of these cases, and they urged action. The swift bipartisan passage of this bill through Congress this year indicates a strong consensus that the suffering of two victims can never equal only one offense.[111]

In his speech, the president also noted that, by recognizing unborn victims, "we reaffirm that the United States of America is building a culture of life."[112] During deliberations on UVVA, supporters had criticized the single-victim Motherhood Protection Act's language as disrespectful to human life. Serrin Foster had testified:

> Instead of recognizing a woman's unborn child as an additional victim, [the Motherhood Protection Act] would "provide additional punishment for certain crimes against women when the crimes cause an interruption in the normal course of their pregnancies."
>
> An "interruption?" That implies something temporary, as if it were possible for the victim's pregnancy to start back up again. . . . Motherhood is neither protected nor honored through the proposed Motherhood Protection Act.[113]

Concerns about abortion rights are invalid.

Pro-choice advocates have criticized both UVVA and state fetal homicide laws as a threat to abortion rights, despite the fact that UVVA explicitly excludes abortion. The House Judiciary Committee flatly rejected such concerns, finding that:

> [UVVA] does not affect, nor in any way interfere with, a woman's right to abort a pregnancy. Indeed, the bill clearly states that it does not apply to "conduct relating to an abortion for which the consent of the pregnant woman, or a person authorized by law to act on her behalf, has been obtained or for which such consent is implied by law." . . . Similarly, the bill also clearly states that it does not permit prosecution "of any woman with respect to her unborn child."[114]

In her Congressional testimony, Foster pointed out that for years laws have recognized unborn children as people with legal rights in various contexts, yet abortion has remained legal. She explained:

> [Outside] the context of abortion, unborn children are often recognized as persons who warrant the law's protection. Most states, for example, allow recovery in one form or another for prenatal injuries. Roughly half the states criminalize fetal homicide. Unborn children have long been recognized as persons for purposes of inheritance, and a child unborn at the time of his or her father's wrongful death has been held to be among the children for whose benefit a wrongful death action may be brought. Federal law similarly recognizes the unborn child as a human subject deserving protection from harmful research.[115]

Some conservatives have suggested that, because of the dire need for fetal homicide laws and the grief caused to the victims and their families, legislators should not allow abortion politics to interfere with the need to "do the right thing." Columnist

Maggie Gallagher criticized Senator John Kerry for his vote against UVVA. She asked rhetorically, "Isn't there something profoundly unattractive about a man who can see a pregnant woman brutally attacked and worry about abortion politics? That's a cold man."[116]

Some pro-life advocates unabashedly admit that unborn victim laws *do* undermine the right to abortion, but they nevertheless do not pose a constitutional problem. Rather than contravening the *holding* of *Roe* v. *Wade*—that women have a constitutional right to choose abortion in certain circumstances—unborn victim laws help to erode the *premise* of the Court's holding—that laws do not recognize an unborn child as a person. The Court did not say that laws cannot recognize an unborn child as a person, and as a democratic nation, pro-life supporters argue, the people should be able to change the laws to correlate with their beliefs.

> • **Does the fact that UVVA specifically exempts abortion guarantee that it will have no impact on abortion?**

Jay Sekulow of the ACLJ asked, "Why is it murder in one case and in another case it's a right enshrined in stone in the Constitution?"[117] He rejected the distinction that an abortion is a voluntary termination of a pregnancy but that a fetal homicide is a crime committed against the woman's will. He argued that the two should both be recognized as the unlawful taking of a human life because "it's not voluntary for the unborn child" in either case.[118]

Every unborn child deserves equal protection from violence.

Some opponents of unborn victim laws have argued that including embryos and fetuses in earlier stages of development is unfair, for the assailant—and maybe even the woman—would have no way of knowing about the pregnancy. Supporters of the laws say that knowledge of the pregnancy is irrelevant to determining the seriousness of the crime. During deliberations over UVVA, Gerard Bradley argued that concerns that UVVA "unfairly penalizes a criminal for the possibly unforeseeable effects of his acts" are invalid.[119] He acknowledged, "in some cases an assailant charged under [UVVA] might not know that his victim is pregnant," but he also pointed out that, in criminal law, violators are "obliged to take their victims as they find them."[120] In other words, if a criminal act does more damage than the criminal intended, the criminal is responsible for all of the damage. Bradley explained:

> The classic expression of this common feature of criminal liability is the "egg-shell skull" rule. Consider A and B, who knock C and D, respectively, over the head with a glass. C is a veteran boxer, and is scarcely dazed. A is thus guilty of, at most, misdemeanor assault and gets a conditional discharge. D has a plate in his head due to an old sports injury, and dies from a brain hemorrhage. B is guilty of homicide, probably manslaughter, and goes to jail for a long time.[121]

Pro-life advocates were pleased with UVVA's final language, which protects an unborn child "at any stage of development, who is carried in the womb."[122] Many states, however, continue to set later benchmarks for when a child is protected under unborn victim laws. Some states recognize a crime against an unborn child only after the end of the embryonic stage, quickening (the detection of movement), or viability. Arguing that fetal homicide laws should recognize the death of an unborn child from conception onward, a justice of the Supreme Court of Kentucky wrote:

> Except for certain superficial differences, there is no meaningful distinction between the unborn child with functioning but younger organs and another unborn child, a few days or weeks older with functioning slightly more advanced. There is

no difference sufficient to justify granting greater consideration to the child in the later stages of development than the
child in the earlier stages. There is no good reason why we
should discriminate against unborn children and treat their
cases any differently than those of any other human being.[123]

Addressing pro-choice concerns that proving the cause of a
miscarriage of an embryo or early-stage fetus is too difficult, the
justice explained:

Prosecution of such behavior should be measured in the
same way as all other questions of fact: 1) by introducing
competent causation evidence established by a preponder-
ance of the evidence in civil cases and beyond a reasonable
doubt in criminal cases and, 2) having the case submitted to
a jury just as any other factual dispute in our legal system.
Unborn children should be treated in the same manner as
other human beings.[124]

> • **Is it possible to prove beyond a reasonable doubt that a
> person caused a woman's miscarriage when as many as one
> in four pregnancies end in miscarriages and many women
> miscarry before they even know that they are pregnant?**

Summary

Pro-life advocates believe that a violent attack against a pregnant
woman is also an attack against her unborn child—two separate
crimes with two separate victims. They argue that considering
such a crime as an attack only on the woman is an affront to the
dignity of human life. Many believe that unborn victim laws
should cover an unborn child from conception onward rather
than from viability onward, as many state laws do.

Laws That Regulate the Conduct of Pregnant Women Invade Their Privacy

In 1987, Angela Carder lay in critical condition at George Washington University Hospital. Her doctors gave her little chance of surviving a lung tumor, even though she had battled cancer for more than half her life since first being diagnosed at age 13. The best that they could offer her was to help ease her pain. Angela was nearing her twenty-seventh week of pregnancy, however, and doctors thought that her unborn child had a chance of survival, especially if Angela lived long enough to reach the twenty-eighth week of her pregnancy. Although pain medication did pose some risk to the fetus, Angela agreed to take it and have the medical care needed to extend her life until the twenty-eighth week.

Unfortunately, Angela's condition worsened and a tube had to be inserted into her throat to help her breathe. She had lost consciousness, and when it looked as though she might die before delivering her baby naturally, the hospital called a judge in the middle of the night, seeking an order allowing doctors to deliver the baby surgically via cesarean section. The hospital needed a court order to perform the C-section because Angela had not agreed to the operation. During a midnight hearing at the hospital, the judge appointed attorneys both for Angela and the fetus and allowed the District of Columbia's lawyers to participate on behalf of the fetus, as well. An obstetrician called to the stand as an expert witness testified that the baby, if delivered then, would have a 50 to 60 percent chance of survival but that delaying the delivery would greatly reduce the chances of survival. Witnesses also testified, however, that the operation would probably hasten Angela's inevitable death. The judge then ordered that C-section be performed.

Soon afterward, Angela regained consciousness, and the doctors told her of the judge's decision. The doctors returned to the impromptu courtroom set up in the hospital, and one testified:

> She does not make sound because of the tube in her windpipe. She nods and she mouths words. One can see what she's saying rather readily. She asked whether she would survive the operation. She asked [Dr.] Hamner if he would perform the operation. He told her he would only perform it if she authorized it but it would be done in any case. She understood that. She then seemed to pause for a few moments and then very clearly mouthed words several times, *I don't want it done. I don't want it done.* Quite clear to me.[125]

Angela's intent was not quite as clear to the judge, who ruled that, because Angela was in such a stressful situation, she could not make an informed decision. The judge reaffirmed the order that the C-section be performed. The operation was not a success. The baby died within two hours of birth, and Angela died two days later.

• Is it appropriate for courts to ignore the wishes of a dying person?

Although nothing could be done to change the course of events, Angela's family pursued the case to help vindicate her rights. An appeals court threw out the trial judge's order and issued a ruling *In re A.C.* to clarify the District of Columbia's law in this area:

> [Every] person has the right, under the common law and the Constitution, to accept or refuse medical treatment. This right of bodily integrity belongs equally to persons who are competent and persons who are not. Further, it matters not what the quality of a patient's life may be; the right of bodily integrity is not extinguished simply because someone is ill, or even at death's door. To protect that right against intrusion by others—family members, doctors, hospitals, or anyone else, however well-intentioned—we hold that a court must determine the patient's wishes by any means available, and must abide by those wishes unless there are truly extraordinary or compelling reasons to override them. When the patient is incompetent, or when the court is unable to determine competency, the substituted judgment procedure must be followed [to determine the patient's own wishes].[126]

Although the appeals court's ruling clarified the law in the District of Columbia and is based on long-standing legal traditions, feminists and pro-choice advocates fear that judges, doctors, hospital administrators, and prosecutors are being given too much power over women's pregnancies. They argue that the woman should have sole discretion over decisions that affect both her embryo or fetus and herself.

Feminists and pro-choice advocates have sharply criticized efforts to "protect the welfare of unborn children," saying that such efforts infringe on the privacy of pregnant women. For example, seeking out and prosecuting pregnant drug users means that pregnant women are subjected to a level of scrutiny not applied to other citizens. Medical procedures—such as C-sections—performed because doctors think that they are in the best interest of the fetus are not always in the best interest of the pregnant woman. Appointing legal representation to a fetus necessarily affects the freedom of the woman carrying the fetus. Feminists and pro-choice advocates have been fighting these battles for years, with mixed results.

> • **Do you think that women are at a disadvantage when dealing with the legal and medical professions?**

Singling out pregnant women for substance use enforcement is discriminatory and dangerous.

Feminists and pro-choice advocates will readily admit that using certain substances during pregnancy poses obstacles to delivering a healthy baby. A great deal of attention has focused on cocaine users giving birth to "crack babies," but the use of legal substances, especially alcohol and tobacco, also poses a significant risk. Uniformly, doctors attempt to dissuade patients from use of alcohol, tobacco, and illegal drugs, suggesting that they seek treatment if they are unable to "kick the habit" on their own. Some doctors, however, in cooperation with legal authorities, have used the threat of jail time as a way to scare women about use of harmful substances. The medical profession and women's advocates have criticized such prosecutions as discriminatory and point out that worries about prosecution prevent women from seeking treatment.

Ground zero in the battle over prosecuting pregnant women for substance use has been Charleston, South Carolina. In the late 1980s, the staff of the Medical University of South Carolina began to notice an increase in the number of cocaine users seeking prenatal care. Although the doctors referred pregnant women to substance abuse programs when appropriate, the rate of cocaine use remained high. The hospital, in conjunction with local prosecutor Charles Condon (who later became the state's attorney general), began a program to prosecute pregnant women who used drugs. The hospital staff already collected urine samples from all pregnant women for medical tests, and they began to screen samples for cocaine use if they suspected that the woman might use cocaine. All positive results were reported to police, and women who tested positive were required to report to a substance abuse treatment program. Prosecutors would file charges only if a woman tested positive a second time or if she failed to attend the substance abuse program. In 1997, the Supreme Court of South Carolina upheld the criminal child neglect conviction of a woman who used crack cocaine during her pregnancy.[127]

> • **Why should someone defend a person who uses illegal drugs during pregnancy?**

In 2001, women's advocates won a battle in the war against South Carolina's prosecution of women for substance use during pregnancy. In *Ferguson* v. *City of Charleston*, the U.S. Supreme Court ruled that Charleston's program of drug testing urine samples taken for medical purposes, without the woman's consent, was unconstitutional. The Court found that the testing of urine samples in cooperation with police authorities constituted an "unreasonable search" in violation of the Fourth Amendment to the U.S. Constitution, which (with certain exceptions) requires police to obtain a search warrant before gathering evidence of a suspected crime. Justice John Paul Stevens, who rejected the city's argument that the testing was justified in the interest of public health, wrote:

> As [city and hospital officials] have repeatedly insisted, their motive was benign rather than punitive. Such a motive, however, cannot justify a departure from Fourth Amendment protections, given the pervasive involvement of law enforcement with the development and application of the . . . policy. The stark and unique fact that characterizes this case is that [the testing] was designed to obtain evidence of criminal conduct by the tested patients that would be turned over to the police and that could be admissible in subsequent criminal

prosecutions. While respondents are correct that drug abuse both was and is a serious problem, "the gravity of the threat alone cannot be dispositive of questions concerning what means law enforcement officers may employ to pursue a given purpose." . . . The Fourth Amendment's general prohibition against nonconsensual, warrantless, and suspicionless searches necessarily applies to such a policy.[128]

Although opponents of drug testing won this particular battle, the war continued. Nothing in the Supreme Court's ruling prohibited hospitals from seeking a warrant to test a urine sample for drugs if a doctor or nurse suspected a pregnant patient of using drugs. More practically, hospitals could simply bury a sentence about drug testing in the paperwork that its patients sign when they seek care. Indeed, South Carolina prosecutors continued to prosecute women for using drugs during pregnancy, including charging women who abused substances with homicide if their children were stillborn. In 2003, the South Carolina Supreme Court upheld the homicide conviction of a woman, Regina McKnight, who had used cocaine during her pregnancy and then gave birth to a stillborn baby.[129]

Although other state courts have generally rejected the position of South Carolina courts, prosecutors nationwide have tried to prosecute women for using drugs, including alcohol, during pregnancy. Prosecutors in Glens Falls, New York, charged Stacey Gilligan with child endangerment after her baby allegedly was born drunk—that is, with a blood alcohol level more than twice the legal limit permitted for driving. Civil liberties advocates, including the New York Civil Liberties Union, came to Gilligan's assistance, and the charges were dropped.

> • **Does it make sense to target illegal drug use but not alcohol use for prosecution?**

Although they acknowledge that drug and alcohol use during pregnancy poses health risks to an embryo or fetus, opponents of prosecutions raise numerous objections. They say that testing programs are discriminatory, that they discourage women from getting proper health care, and that they infringe on women's childbearing rights.

One of the major objections to testing and prosecuting pregnant women for drug and alcohol use is that doing so singles out women in a discriminatory way. Use of cocaine, marijuana, and various other substances is illegal for everyone, but the government does not submit all citizens to drug testing. Similarly, people are not tested for alcohol use, and even adults who drink too much are not prosecuted unless they violate some other law, such as driving while drunk.

By scrutinizing the behavior of pregnant women and singling them out for drug and alcohol testing, the law is treating pregnant women differently than it treats other adults. Critics say that this differential treatment amounts to discrimination. In the case of State v. McKnight, the South Carolina chapter of NOW argued:

> A pregnant addict's ability to cease drug use is, at best, identical to that of her male counterpart, yet the State's prosecution of pregnant women treats them as though their physical and mental inability to stop their addiction is motivated by an intent to deliver drugs to their fetuses, and thus requires punishment by the State. This prosecution deprives women of their most basic liberty based on unfounded and improper stereotypes of women and pregnancy.[130]

Some have charged that the prosecutions are discriminatory in other ways, such as focusing on poor, African-American women. Rachel Roth pointed out that, nationally, "[in] cases in which the woman's race is known, 71 percent were Black, Latina, or Native American; only 29 percent were white . . . . [In South Carolina] almost all the women are Black."[131] Lynn Paltrow of National Advocates for Pregnant Women (NAPW) commented, "[Many] African-American women [have been] dragged out of [a] predominantly black hospital in chains and shackles, evoking sharp modern images of black women in slavery."[132]

Roth also noted that most prosecutions involved women who used crack cocaine. She and others have charged this pattern of prosecuting so-called "crack moms" is based on societal prejudices fueled by the media. "Newspaper photos show pregnant women smoking crack cocaine, with teddy bears and other children's toys thrown to the floor at their feet," wrote Cynthia Daniels.[133] As a result, wrote Paltrow:

> Pregnant women became an appealing target for law enforcement officials who were losing the war on drugs. . . . Pregnant drug-using women, portrayed as depraved, inner-city African-American women who voluntarily ingested crack to poison their children, were not likely to receive much support from a public that had been convinced by sensational news reports that crack use during pregnancy inevitably caused significant and irreparable damage to the developing fetus.[134]

Despite the media frenzy, medical research suggests that use of crack cocaine during pregnancy is not a significantly greater risk than use of other illegal drugs or even alcohol and tobacco, both of which are legal substances. In the *McKnight* case, the South Carolina Medical Association (SCMA) and other groups argued:

> Low birth weight, sudden infant death syndrome, spontaneous abortion, premature rupture of the membranes, and abnormal placentation are all well-established consequences associated with prenatal tobacco exposure, and it is widely accepted by medical researchers that smoking during pregnancy substantially increases the risk of stillbirth. By contrast, cocaine—while not benign—does not cause "the frank damage found with nicotine or smoking."[135]

Roth concluded, "[The] decision to focus on prosecuting pregnant women who use crack is a decision to target poor Black women, one that cannot be justified medically but can be justified politically and ideologically."[136]

Although South Carolina has defended its prosecutions of pregnant women as a legal weapon needed to get some women into drug or alcohol treatment programs, many people believe that the prosecutions do little in this regard. In *McKnight*, the SCMA argued:

> Because addicted individuals are physically and psychologically dependent on the substance to which they are addicted, and their addiction may well have biologic and genetic underpinnings, they are often unable to stop using the drug without outside assistance. . . . More importantly, because of the compulsive nature of drug dependency, criminal sanctions are unlikely to achieve the goal of deterring drug use among pregnant women, but instead will only act to further demonize them.[137]

Some critics point out that many pregnant women might be interested in substance abuse treatment programs but that such programs are not adequately funded or publicized. In the *Gilligan* case, the NYCLU and other groups pointed out that women faced two significant barriers in gaining access to alcohol and drug treatment programs. First, many programs have refused to accept pregnant women as patients. Second, many programs do not accept Medicaid, the government-sponsored health insurance program that covers many low-income women. Women also faced other obstacles, such as lack of childcare, which prevented them from participating in alcohol and drug treatment programs. The groups argued, "The prosecution of Ms. Gilligan for failing to overcome her alcohol dependency while pregnant . . . disregards the unfortunate fact that Ms. Gilligan and many women like her simply cannot access appropriate treatment through no fault of their own."[138]

Many medical authorities believe that threatening pregnant women with prosecution for drug use is not only ineffective but also dangerous. In the *McKnight* case, the SCMA pointed out that, in the years since the state's Supreme Court first upheld the conviction of a woman for using drugs during pregnancy, in *Whitner* v. *State*, the participation of pregnant women in substance abuse programs had dropped. The group attributed the drop in participation to fear of prosecution, arguing:

> The *Whitner* decision is producing real and dire consequences for pregnant women in South Carolina, many of whom now avoid prenatal care and drug and alcohol treatment for fear that confiding their health problems to their physicians or counselors could lead to their arrest and imprisonment and the removal of their children from their care.[139]

Critics say that fear of prosecution has a much broader public health impact than a drop in participation in substance abuse treatment. The fear also deters pregnant women from seeking any type of medical care. Even without the threat of prosecution, many pregnant women who have substance abuse problems do not seek the prenatal care necessary to ensure the delivery of a healthy baby. The SCMA argued that the fear of prosecution had only made the problem worse: "South Carolina recorded its most significant increase in infant mortality in a decade in 1997. This increase coincided with the *Whitner* decision and the publicity surrounding it."[140]

Some pro-choice advocates are concerned about the broader implications of prosecuting women for substance abuse during pregnancy. In a law review article that criticized the *Whitner* decision, Lynn Paltrow argued that the decision "[provides] support to the anti-abortion position that fetuses have rights and that the pregnant woman's health and freedom may be subordinated to those rights."[141] In her opinion, in order to protect women's right to make decisions about abortion and childbearing, pro-choice advocates "must be willing to defend the rights of all women including women who use drugs."[142]

Women have the right to make their own medical decisions, even if their decisions put a fetus at risk.

Another area in which feminists and pro-choice advocates have criticized efforts to expand fetal rights is in the context of making choices as maternity patient. Doctors and hospitals often pressure women to undergo treatments that primarily benefit the fetus, and most women follow the advice. Some women do not want to follow the advice of their doctors, however, and advocates say that a woman should have an absolute right to make her own medical decisions, even if her decision puts a fetus at risk.

Generally, an adult has the right to refuse any unwanted medical treatment, and health care providers must receive informed consent for all treatments given. What this means is that the provider is required to inform the patient of all of the benefits and risks of a particular treatment, such as surgery or a vaccination, and the patient must give permission to the provider. This right developed out of legal traditions inherited from British law, and the U.S. Supreme Court has recognized that "a competent person has a constitutionally protected liberty interest in refusing unwanted medical treatment."[143] In most cases, the person who is making the decision is the only person affected, and therefore the right is absolute. Doctors and hospitals have frequently sought help from a court system in forcing women to submit to particular treatments, however, on the basis that the woman's decision affects the life and health of the fetus.

A number of situations exist in which pregnant women wish to refuse medical care recommended by their doctors. For example, when doctors recommend that a cesarean section is necessary to prevent death or grave harm to a fetus, women do not always want to follow that advice. They might not agree that the surgery is necessary, or they might simply wish to avoid

30 years of legal battles for abortion

Outside of Supreme Court rulings, many states have their own laws regarding abortion including 24-hour waiting periods and mandatory consent for minors.

Jan. 22, 1973–Roe v. Wade: abortion legalized.

1981–Bellotti v. Baird: a pregnant minor can petition a court for permission to have an abortion without parental notification.

1989–Webster v. Reproductive Health Services: gives states significant rights to regulate abortion.

1992–Planned Parenthood of Southeastern Pennsylvania v. Casey: reaffirms a woman's right to end pregnancy in early stages and makes it clear that a total ban on abortion would be found un-constitutional.

1995–The 104th Congress passes a bill to outlaw a late-term procedure that anti-abortion activists call "partial-birth abortion."

1996–President Clinton vetoes 1995 legislation, saying it should include a provision to allow the abortion procedure if needed to protect a woman's health as well as her life. Congress fails to override the veto.

1998–The National Organization for Women uses a racketeering law meant to stop organized crime to convince a federal jury that anti-abortion leaders engaged in a nationwide extortion scheme to shut down clinics.

1999–Ruling orders anti-abortion activists to pay abortion providers $107 million in damages for making illegal threats through listing the doctors' names and addresses on a Web site.

2000–Stenberg v. Carhart: strikes down Nebraska's law banning the late-term abortion procedure.

Jan. 22, 2001–Two days after taking office, President Bush signs an executive order barring U.S. aid to international groups that use their own money to support abortion.

SOURCE: Associated Press   AP

In 1973, *Roe* v. *Wade* made abortion legal throughout the United States. This timeline shows how state laws and court cases have added to the body of law that regulates abortion.

major surgery that requires additional days of hospitalization after the delivery. In addition, delivering by C-section can affect a woman's ability to deliver future babies nonsurgically. Rates of delivery by C-section have risen dramatically in the United States and other countries: Approximately one in four U.S. babies is born by C-section.

> • **Do you know anyone who has chosen not to have a physician deliver her baby in a hospital? What were her reasons?**

The rise in the rate of C-sections has led to a backlash against the procedure. Some have formed interest groups seeking to reduce the rate of cesarean deliveries. Although it acknowledges that certain medical conditions make a C-section medically necessary, the International Cesarean Awareness Network has charged that half of C-sections are performed unnecessarily, jeopardizing women's health.

Generally, courts have upheld women's right to refuse C-sections, as the appeals court did in reversing the order that allowed doctors to perform a C-section on Angela Carder. In that case, however, a C-section was performed, and by the time the appeals court heard the case, Carder and her baby had already died. Trial judges, frequently called in the middle of the night and conducting a quick hearing in a hospital room, have continued to issue orders that allow doctors to perform unwanted C-sections. In 2004, when a Pennsylvania woman refused to have a C-section, a county judge approved an order that gave the hospital guardianship over her fetus and allowed the hospital to perform a C-section against the woman's will. The woman had already left the hospital rather than submit to the C-section. As she explained to a local newspaper, she had a friend who had died as the result of a C-section and she believed that she could deliver the baby without a C-section, as she had done with her six previous children.[144] The woman successfully delivered a healthy baby at another hospital—without a C-section—and she and her husband were outraged by the first hospital's actions.

Although less common, another scenario in which women have rejected treatments deemed necessary by a doctor is the refusal of a blood transfusion by a woman who is a Jehovah's Witness. People of that faith believe that accepting a blood transfusion is a violation of biblical law that can lead to expulsion from the church and prevent salvation. Women can experience hemorrhaging— severe bleeding—as an uncommon but serious complication of pregnancy, and, if serious enough, the bleeding can threaten the life of both the woman and her fetus. Jehovah's Witnesses routinely reject transfusions, even in life-threatening situations.

> • **Should a woman be required to demonstrate that her objections to a medical procedure are based on religious beliefs, or should she be allowed to make the decision for personal reasons?**

An Illinois appeals court ruled in the case *In re: Brown* that a judge erred in issuing an order that required a woman to undergo a blood transfusion against her will:

> [In] balancing the mother's right to refuse medical treatment against the State's substantial interest in the viable fetus, we hold that the State may not override a pregnant woman's competent treatment decision, including refusal of recommended invasive medical procedures, to potentially save the life of the viable fetus. We . . . find that a blood transfusion is an invasive medical procedure that interrupts a competent adult's bodily integrity.[145]

Although the law is clear on the issue of informed consent, pregnant women have frequently found themselves involved in legal battles to refuse treatment. It is worth noting that both the *A.C.* and *Brown* decisions involved appeals courts overturning judges' orders of procedures that had already been performed. Carder was subjected to surgery against her wishes, and both she and her baby died soon afterward. Brown was subjected to a transfusion, and although she and her baby were physically healthy, her religious choice was violated.

In general, the medical field recognizes that a pregnant woman's choice of treatment should be definitive, even if her decision poses risks to the fetus. The American College of Obstetricians and Gynecologists (ACOG) cites both medical and ethical reasons for advising its members not to force unwanted treatments on patients. Medically speaking, existing diagnostic techniques limit physicians' ability to predict with absolute certainty that a fetus faces health risks, and the unwanted medical procedure does not always produce the desired results.[146] In the case of the Pennsylvania woman, the C-section evidently was not absolutely necessary, and in Angela Carder's case, the court-ordered C-section was not successful in preserving the baby's life. Ethically speaking, ACOG urges members not to perform an unwanted procedure or to seek a court order to allow one. Not only do such actions "[violate] the pregnant woman's autonomy," but also could produce the undesirable result of "criminalization of noncompliance with medical recommendations."[147]

Some in the medical field have used the term "maternal-fetal conflict" to describe cases such as Carder's and Brown's and increasingly speak of a fetus as a "second patient." Rachel Roth rejects the use of the term "maternal-fetal conflict," writing that the conflict that exists is "between women and medical authority and between women and state authority."[148] Cynthia Daniels wrote that viewing the fetus as a second patient jeopardizes women's rights and that, as pro-life advocates publicized cases in which pregnant women refused treatment, "The pregnant woman was now cast as the person who stood *between* the physician and the 'patient.'"[149] In other words, she wrote, the mother loses her identity as a person and as a patient, and is "transformed into a vehicle of fetal interests."[150]

Many feminists are concerned that, as a woman's right to refuse medical treatment is called into question, politicians will develop new methods to restrict women's behavior during pregnancy. Roth wrote, "Each year scientists continue to identify more and more possible ways to lower health risks to fetuses. . . . Without concerted opposition, political conservatives can take these new findings as a basis for restricting women's lives. . . ."[151] She discussed other examples of behaviors and actions that pose some degree of risk to an unborn fetus, such as flying on an airplane or working in industrial settings, and noted that restricting women's ability to engage in such activities limits their life opportunities in ways that men are not limited.

Criminal justice Professor Robert Costello suggested that prosecuting women for cocaine use during pregnancy sets a dangerous precedent because the activities that could be targeted for prosecution are almost limitless. Among the activities that could be prosecuted are "lack of sleep, inadequate diet, obsessive use of caffeine products, taking prescription and over the counter medications, physical duress, [and] lack of physical fitness."[152]

- **Should an unborn child have a separate doctor who makes recommendations on what is best for it?**

The appointment of a fetal guardian jeopardizes a woman's health and autonomy.

One method that hospitals and pro-life advocates have used to force women to undergo unwanted medical procedures has been to ask the court to appoint a guardian or an attorney for the fetus. In the recent Pennsylvania case and in the Angela Carder case, the judge who ordered the C-section appointed someone to represent the fetus's legal interests separately from the pregnant woman's legal interests. Feminists and pro-choice advocates have vigorously opposed such appointment of legal guardians.

Courts typically appoint a guardian to represent the rights of a person who cannot, for various reasons, legally make his or her own decisions. The court might appoint a guardian for someone who is in a coma and cannot make any type of decision. If a court believes that someone cannot make rational decisions because of mental retardation, dementia, or a mental illness, it might appoint a guardian to make more rational decisions. In the case of minors, even those who are old enough to make relatively intelligent choices, laws may prevent them from making certain decisions, such as signing contracts or consenting to medical treatment. Usually, a parent serves as the minor's legal guardian in these situations, but, in some cases, judges rule that a parent's decisions are detrimental to a child and appoint a separate guardian. A common example is appointing a guardian when parents refuse medical treatment for a child, although such appointments remain controversial.

Appointing a guardian for a fetus is even more controversial. Typically, a pregnant woman makes decisions that affect both her own health and that of her fetus, and in cases in which the mother is incompetent, the court appoints a guardian for the woman to make medical decisions. A controversy in Florida captured headlines in 2004, as pro-life Governor Jeb Bush's administration supported efforts to have a guardian appointed to represent a fetus carried by a young woman with significant mental disabilities.

J.D.S. had numerous disabilities, including severe mental retardation, cerebral palsy, autism, and seizure disorder. She was raped while living in a group home for people with developmental disabilities, and she became pregnant. Because she could not communicate or fully understand her situation, the court appointed a guardian to act in her interest and make medical decisions related to her pregnancy, which could have included a decision to have an abortion. The guardian decided that J.D.S. would carry her baby to term. Nevertheless, the Jeb Bush administration intervened and sought to have a separate guardian appointed to represent the fetus's rights. One particular area of concern was that J.D.S. took psychotropic medications to treat her mental disabilities, and these medications can pose a risk to fetal development.

A coalition of pro-choice organizations filed a brief in the case. The groups argued that the medical conflicts, such as the decision whether a pregnant woman should continue to take medications that helped her but could harm the fetus, had to be left to the woman's discretion. Their brief stated:

> When, as here, a woman chooses to carry to term, she will need to make medical treatment decisions that may have an impact on the fetus; if a guardian is appointed for the fetus, her ability to make those private medical decisions during her pregnancy will necessarily be impaired and her health may be jeopardized by the fetal guardian's advocacy for medical choices beneficial to the fetus but detrimental to the woman's health.[153]

The fact that J.D.S. was not capable of making her own decisions was irrelevant, the groups argued, noting that, legally speaking, J.D.S. *was* making her own decisions, albeit through her guardian, who was legally bound to make decisions in the best interest of J.D.S. The groups argued:

> Appointing a guardian for a fetus would directly infringe upon a woman's constitutional [rights]. . . . This is no less true in the case of a pregnant woman who has been determined to be legally incompetent and for whom a guardian has been appointed; such a woman is entitled to exercise her constitutional rights and medical choices through her court-appointed guardian. Thus, appointment of a guardian for the fetus here would violate the constitutional rights of J.D.S., just as such an appointment would violate the constitutional rights of any other pregnant woman.[154]

The groups noted that appointment of a legal guardian would also interfere with a woman's constitutionally protected right to choose an abortion. Their brief stated:

> Appointment of a guardian for a fetus would . . . violate established constitutional norms. It would create an automatic adversary to a woman genuinely considering abortion as an

option and to a woman carrying to term and considering any medical care detrimental to the fetus, and would ensure vigorous opposition to any potential decision that could risk harm to the fetus. Such a situation would permit a third party to substantially intrude on a woman's reproductive health decisions—including the decision whether to have an abortion and how to carry to term—and impose risks to the woman's health and well-being. This is plainly unconstitutional. Prior to viability, the decision whether to continue a pregnancy

FROM THE BENCH

Florida Appeals Court Denies Appointment of a Fetal Guardian

A Florida court turned down the appeal of a woman, Jennifer Wixtrom, who sought to be appointed the legal guardian of a fetus carried by another woman, J.D.S., who had severe mental disabilities. In rejecting the appeal, which had been backed by Governor Jeb Bush's administration, the court noted that Florida law does not recognize a fetus as a "person."

Jennifer Wixtrom appeals an order denying her petition to be appointed guardian of the fetus of J.D.S., an incapacitated female. We conclude that the trial court correctly denied the petition and affirm. . . .

Section 744.102(8), Florida Statues, defines a "guardian" as "a person who has been appointed by the court to act on behalf of a ward's person or property or both." A " 'ward' means a *person* for whom a guardian has been appointed." § 744.102(19), Fla. Stat. (emphasis added). It follows that a fetus must be considered a "person" to be appointed a guardian. We find no Florida statute or case law that has determined a fetus to be a person. Rather, the opposite is true. For instance, the Florida Supreme Court declined to rule that a fetus is a "person" within the meaning of the Florida Wrongful Death Act, 8 *Young v. St. Vincent's Medical Center, Inc.*, 673 So. 2d 482, 483 (Fla. 1996), and the Fourth District declined to apply a child abuse statute 9 in a case involving a fetus, *State v. Gethers*, 585 So. 2d 1140 (Fla. 4th DCA 1991). See also *Roe v. Wade*, 410 U.S. 113, 158 (1973) ("the word 'person,' as used in the Fourteenth Amendment, does not include the unborn").

Source: *In re: Guardianship of J.D.S.*, NO. 5D03-1921 (Fla. 5th D.C.A., Jan. 9, 2004).

rests entirely with the woman; after viability, not only does a woman retain the right to decide whether to carry to term if doing so would pose a risk to her health or life, but her health is entitled to overriding consideration with respect to her medical treatment throughout her pregnancy.[155]

A Florida appeals court upheld a trial judge's refusal to appoint a guardian for the fetus carried by J.D.S. The court did not address the constitutional issues raised by the pro-choice groups, instead ruling that the plain meaning of the state's guardianship laws did not cover guardians for fetuses. It ruled, "We conclude that the absence of a provision for fetuses means that the protection of the statute does not extend to fetuses."[156] Despite the favorable rulings in the J.D.S. and Angela Carder cases, the issue came up later in Pennsylvania and will probably come up again; therefore, pro-choice advocates remain poised to contest fetal guardianship cases.

> • **Does the unborn child of a mentally incompetent woman need a guardian any more than the unborn child of any other woman? Is this the reason pro-choice groups were so concerned about the *J.D.S.* case?**

Summary

Many feminists and pro-choice advocates believe that pregnant women should have the right to make their own decisions, even when the decisions pose a risk to an embryo or fetus. They do not condone illegal drug use, but they argue that singling out pregnant women for drug testing amounts to discrimination and will deter pregnant drug-users from getting proper prenatal care. They also believe that forcing unwanted treatments on a woman for the benefit of an embryo or fetus is a violation of her privacy and often has disastrous results.

In Some Cases, the Law Must Protect Unborn Children From Their Mothers' Behavior

In 2004, Melissa Ann Rowland delivered twins in a Utah hospital. One of the twins was stillborn. Circumstances surrounding the incident are murky, but various press accounts reported that Rowland had a history of mental illness and had used cocaine during her pregnancy. Prosecutors alleged that the stillbirth was caused by her refusal—some time before the births—to have an immediate cesarean section. Rowland eventually did give birth by cesarean section and publicly denied having refused an earlier C-section.

Prosecutors charged Rowland with murder in the stillbirth of the twin. The basis for the charges was allegations by hospital staff that Rowland's earlier refusal of a C-section had led to the stillbirth of the twin. It was also alleged that the basis of her refusal was that she did not want the scar left by the operation. Prosecutors charged that her "depraved indifference" to life led to the stillbirth.

Ultimately, Rowland pleaded guilty to two charges of child endangerment, an offense that carries a much lighter sentence than murder. The plea agreement drew widespread condemnation from feminists and pro-choice advocates, who accused prosecutors of jeopardizing women's right to make medical decisions. It was Rowland's own actions that drew outrage from pro-life advocates, many of whom applauded the prosecutor's actions. Conservative columnist Jennifer Graham lamented, "Every day, we see mothers willing to put their kids second (or third or fourth) in ways that shock and repel us." [157]

Another case that shocked and repelled many people was that of Regina McKnight. In 1999, McKnight's daughter was stillborn, and tests revealed evidence of cocaine in the baby's body, indicating that McKnight had used cocaine during her pregnancy. Had the baby survived, it might have been considered a miracle. Her court records show that she was homeless, smoked a pack of cigarettes per day, and suffered from syphilis, a serious sexually transmitted infection, as well as other medical conditions. Pathologists testified that McKnight's cocaine use was the cause of her daughter's death.

A South Carolina court convicted her of murder by child abuse, and the South Carolina Supreme Court upheld the conviction, ruling:

> McKnight admitted she knew she was pregnant and that she had been using cocaine when she could get it, primarily on weekends. Given the fact that it is public knowledge that usage of cocaine is potentially fatal, we find the fact that McKnight took cocaine knowing she was pregnant was sufficient evidence to [find that] she acted with extreme indifference to her child's life.[158]

The U.S. Supreme Court refused to hear McKnight's appeal, and many conservatives praised the ruling. Wendy Wright of Concerned Women for America said, "By taking an illegal drug, she not only was harming herself—which the law recognizes as being an illegal act—but also ended up hurting an innocent human being." [159]

Cases like Rowland's and McKnight's, pro-life advocates say, are reminders that some women cannot be trusted to keep their children's best interest in mind. Brushing aside pro-choice arguments that women should be allowed to make their own decisions about their lifestyle and medical treatment, pro-life advocates argue that some unborn children need protection from their mothers' dangerous behavior and risky medical decisions. They argue that, in some cases, an unborn child needs legal representation in order to ensure this protection.

> • It is said, "Hard cases make bad law." Should headline-grabbing stories set legal standards for every woman, including those who are generally law abiding?

Maternal use of alcohol, tobacco, and other drugs threatens an unborn child's life and health.

Medical research shows that the use of alcohol, tobacco, and other drugs during pregnancy pose great risks to the healthy development of an unborn child. According to a fact sheet published by the National Clearinghouse for Alcohol and Drug Information, a federal agency:

- Heavy alcohol consumption by a pregnant woman can result in her child being born with fetal alcohol syndrome (FAS), the leading known environmental cause of mental retardation in the Western World. According to research estimates, 1–3 of every 1,000 babies are born with FAS.

- There is no known safe level of alcohol consumption for a pregnant woman. Pregnant women who consume between one and two drinks per day are twice as likely as nondrinkers to have low birthweight babies and are at increased risk for miscarrying during the second trimester of pregnancy. Additionally, studies suggest that binge-like drinking, or more drinks in a short amount of time, may be more harmful to the fetus than exposure to the same or larger amounts of alcohol spread out more evenly over time.

- Pregnant women who use drugs such as heroin, methadone, amphetamines, PCP, marijuana, crack, or cocaine can give birth to addicted babies who undergo withdrawal, known as neonatal abstinence syndrome (NAS). Signs of NAS include increased sensitivity to noise, irritability, poor coordination, tremors, and feeding problems. . . .

- Pregnant women who smoke are more likely than nonsmokers to have low birthweight babies and babies who are at risk for developmental delays. Maternal smoking is a contributing factor in 14 percent of premature deliveries in the United States. Additionally, there is a direct correlation between the amount of smoking during pregnancy and the frequency of spontaneous abortion and fetal death.[160]

Almost everyone agrees that everything possible should be done to help pregnant women avoid use of alcohol, tobacco, and other drugs during pregnancy; they differ, however, about the best way to achieve this goal. Many suggest that the answer is increased availability of voluntary treatment programs for pregnant women, and others argue that tougher measures are needed. Some have suggested that other states should adopt South Carolina's tactic of prosecuting pregnant women who use illegal drugs.

In South Carolina, prosecutions have generally been limited to women who use cocaine, as opposed to those who use alcohol and tobacco. Some critics of South Carolina's policy argue that it ignores the fact that alcohol and tobacco are thought to be more harmful to a developing embryo or fetus than cocaine is. From a practical standpoint, however, prosecutors would likely face a more difficult time convincing a jury to convict a woman for using alcohol and tobacco, which are substances that adults are permitted to use.

Advocates of prosecution reject efforts by opponents to downplay the risk that cocaine use poses to an unborn child. In a U.S. Supreme Court case, *Ferguson* v. *City of Charleston*, attorneys for the South Carolina city pointed out the dangers associated with cocaine use:

> Effects on the mothers include: [increased] risk of premature delivery, premature separation of the placenta (abruptio placentae), spontaneous abortion, and death. Cocaine use during pregnancy can affect infants in a number of ways, including an increased risk of sudden death syndrome, low birth weight, seizures, strokes, heart attacks, lack of bonding, emotional disorders, behavioral problems and learning disabilities. . . . In some cases, even a single dose of cocaine can kill the baby and the mother too.[161]

In addition to the harm posed to individual children, the effects of prenatal cocaine use have created a public health problem by imposing costs on the health care system. Former South Carolina Attorney General Charles Condon has noted that the delivery of a healthy baby costs only $500, but the costs associated with the birth of a "crack baby" have reached $750,000. Moreover, "most are born to welfare mothers, so Medicaid and the hospital were picking up the bill," he said.[162] The costs of prenatal cocaine use are also reflected in the cost to society, argued the lawyers for the city of Charleston; these costs include "increased needs for social services, foster care, and special education services, lower levels of achievement of educational and occupational goals, increased family stress, and reduced maternal bonding."[163]

FROM THE BENCH

South Carolina Supreme Court Upholds Conviction for Prenatal Cocaine Use

South Carolina is the only state in which women routinely face prosecution for using drugs during pregnancy. In 1998, the state's Supreme Court upheld the child abuse conviction of a woman whose baby tested positive for traces of cocaine, and the U.S. Supreme Court refused to hear her appeal. The state court based its ruling on South Carolina's recognition of an unborn child as a person.

> On April 20, 1992, Cornelia Whitner (Whitner) pled guilty to criminal child neglect, S.C.Code Ann. § 20-7-50 (1985), for causing her baby to be born with cocaine metabolites in its system by reason of Whitner's ingestion of crack cocaine during the third trimester of her pregnancy....
>
> South Carolina law has long recognized that viable fetuses are persons holding certain legal rights and privileges [and] we do not see any rational basis for finding a viable fetus is not a "person" in the present context. Indeed, it would be absurd to recognize the viable fetus as a person for purposes of homicide laws and wrongful death statutes but not for purposes of statutes proscribing child abuse....
>
> Whitner admits to having ingested crack cocaine during the third trimester of her pregnancy, which caused her child to be born with cocaine in its system. Although the precise effects of maternal crack use during pregnancy are somewhat unclear, it is well documented and within the realm of public knowledge that such use can cause serious harm to the viable unborn child.... There can be no question here Whitner endangered the life, health, and comfort of her child.

Source: Whitner v. State, 328 S.C. 1, 492 S.E.2d 777 (1997), cert. denied 523 U.S. 1145 (1998).

> • **What can be done to reduce substance abuse among pregnant women? Do prevention and treatment programs seem to work for others? Are they likely to be more effective for pregnant women?**

Despite the obvious dangers of substance abuse during pregnancy, South Carolina has been the only state to routinely threaten pregnant substance abusers with prosecution. The Medical University of South Carolina (MUSC) established a program for testing pregnant women for drugs and reporting the results to police. Women then had the choice of drug treatment or prosecution. After the U.S. Supreme Court ruled in *Ferguson* that the secret testing was an unreasonable search in violation of women's constitutional rights, the state has been limited to prosecutions in cases in which drug use is obvious, including those cases in which a child is stillborn. In *State* v. *McKnight*, the state's Supreme Court upheld the conviction of Regina McKnight for the stillbirth of her child, finding that *Ferguson* did not bar her prosecution by the state.

In other states, efforts to prosecute women for substance abuse during pregnancy have been derailed by strong opposition from women's groups and medical providers' associations. Women's groups tend to object on the basis that prosecutions discriminate against women and invade their privacy. Providers' groups argue that the threat of prosecution deters women from seeking prenatal care and that expanding voluntary drug treatment services would be more effective. Proponents of prosecution dismiss these concerns.

The logic behind the pro-choice objection to prosecution seems to be that allowing states to prosecute behavior that harms an unborn child lays the groundwork for prosecuting abortions. Proponents of prosecution point out important differences between drug use and abortion decisions. In *Roe* v. *Wade*, the U.S. Supreme Court recognized that a woman has a right to privacy that includes the right to make decisions about abortion.

Although the Court characterized this right as an important one, it also ruled that a woman's right to choose must be weighed against the state's interest in protecting the life and health of pregnant women and in protecting the life of unborn children. The Court held that, at viability, the state's interest in protecting the life of unborn children outweighs women's right to privacy.

> • **Do people have a right to privacy when it comes to illegal drug use? What about drinking alcohol? Smoking?**

With regard to illegal drug use, the balancing equation is much different: The Court would be forced to weigh the state's interest in preserving life against a woman's interest in using illegal drugs. As Condon pointed out, however, "[People] don't have a right to use crack cocaine; it's a felony."[164] Some people believe that the state's interest in protecting the life of unborn children does not begin at viability and instead exists throughout the pregnancy. Indeed, substance abuse can be especially harmful at the earliest stages of pregnancy. In a law review article, Louise Chan wrote, "It does not follow that because a woman has a legal right to abort her pre-viable fetus, she therefore has a right to engage in illegal conduct that would harm, but not terminate, the fetus."[165]

Proponents of prosecution maintain that arguments about abortion and privacy, despite their lack of substance, have distracted attention from the real issue—protecting unborn children from the effects of substance abuse. Prosecutor Paul Logli noted, "Abuse of drugs by a pregnant mother is met with almost universal condemnation," and blames the "pro-abortion lobby" for subverting the will of the people by blocking legislation that would criminalize substance abuse during pregnancy.[166] He lamented, "Frozen by fear of being labeled sexist, anti-choice, or unenlightened, legislators have refused to consider sanctions that would communicate societal outrage at the illegal behavior of a small group of people engaged in the selfish destruction of their own innocent young."[167]

Condon dismissed charges that South Carolina's enforcement program is racist. He admitted that most of the women forced into treatment by MUSC's testing program were African American, but he explained that the imbalance was the result of circumstance rather than racist intent, noting, "The hospital serves a primarily indigent population, and most of the patient population is black. The South Carolina Drug Prevalence Study showed blacks were more likely to use cocaine than whites." [168] Prosecutor Paul Logli has argued for testing all infants for traces of narcotics at birth.[169] Universal testing would ensure that authorities are not singling out women by race.

Proponents of prosecution argue that the alternative proposed by opponents—expanding the availability of voluntary treatment—simply does not work. Charles Condon noted that the voluntary approach had failed in South Carolina: "At first, the hospital tried to educate the women about the damage they were causing to themselves and to their unborn babies. Sadly, hospital workers could not convince many of the expectant drug-addicted women to enter a drug-treatment program. Most wouldn't even return for any type of prenatal care at all." [170]

In contrast, wrote Condon, South Carolina's threats of prosecution have been very successful in getting women into treatment programs. He argued that the testing program invalidated by the U.S. Supreme Court in the *Ferguson* case, "was not punitive" and "was not designed to put people in jail"; rather, "it was a humanitarian effort to save lives." [171] In fact, he noted, most of the women agreed to enter drug treatment immediately when threatened with prosecution, and most of the others did so after they were arrested.

Pro-choice advocates frequently argue that punishing women for using illegal drugs during pregnancy will lead down a "slippery slope," in which women are prosecuted for using legal substances such as alcohol and tobacco. They point out that alcohol and tobacco use are thought to be more harmful to unborn children than cocaine. Some pro-life advocates agree that prosecuting women for using illegal drugs during pregnancy opens the door to prosecuting women for using alcohol and tobacco but believe that prosecuting women for otherwise legal acts might be necessary to protect unborn children. Praising the South Carolina Supreme Court's ruling in the *McKnight* case, Traditional Values Coalition chairman Reverend Lou Sheldon said that the legal principles of the case "can very well spill over into other kinds of abuses such as alcohol and tobacco." [172]

The welfare of an unborn child outweighs a mother's right to refuse medical treatment.

Although the Melissa Rowland case also involved allegations of prenatal substance abuse, the national public debate sparked by the case focused on the question of whether it is proper to prosecute a woman for refusing to undergo a medical treatment that benefits her unborn child. Many pro-life advocates supported the prosecution and argue that courts should compel a woman to undergo treatments that doctors determine are necessary to protect the life of an unborn child. ACOG took the official position that obstetrician-gynecologists should respect a woman's decision regardless of consequences to the unborn child, but smaller groups of pro-life physicians argue that the welfare of the unborn child should be taken into account.

Bioethicist Scott Rae noted that the legal basis for requiring a pregnant woman to undergo treatment for the benefit of an unborn child is a murky area of the law. On the one hand, courts frequently order treatment for young children against parents' wishes. On the other hand, courts cannot force a parent to provide a life-saving blood transfusion, organ transplant, or bone marrow transplant to the child. Rae distinguished cases that involve forced treatment of a mother for an unborn child's benefit from the latter situation. "The *in utero* relationship is unparalleled in the reliance of the fetus upon the mother. It is not a relationship of strangers, but of total dependence." [173] He suggested, "The argument that one need not undergo risks for which another benefits"—which justifies court's refusal to order the donation of blood, organs, or bone marrow—"may not apply." [174]

Some have suggested that the growing backlash against C-sections overstates the problem. In a column for *National Review*, Jennifer Graham characterized her own experiences delivering all four of her children by C-section in a positive light. Charging that opponents exaggerate the risks and impact of C-sections, Graham wrote, "Pregnancy itself is an invasive procedure." [175] She noted that, before the development of modern medicine, the death rate of women during childbirth was staggering. Although the death rate has dropped to 8 per 100,000 births in the United States, Graham wrote, "Half of these deaths could be prevented through early diagnosis and care. And yes, sometimes that care will include the occasional C-section. Get over it." [176]

> • **Does the increasing percentage of births via C-section indicate that C-sections are being performed unnecessarily?**

Regardless of whether a C-section can be characterized as a major surgery, pro-life advocates reject the idea that a woman's choice whether or not to have the C-section is more important than the life or health of an unborn child. Rae wrote, "The better way to look at this situation is to weigh the *comparative* risk to the fetus and to the mother. When the exercise of a liberty costs someone his or her life, life generally overrides liberty. Cases of forced C-sections can be seen as the conflict between *grave* risk to the fetus and *moderate* risk to the mother." [177] Weighing the risks, Rae concluded that, when a woman refuses a C-section, hospitals are justified in seeking a court order to perform one or, in cases of dire emergency, in performing one without a court order.

Some bioethicists have also argued that the life of an unborn child outweighs a mother's religious liberty. In most cases, courts have upheld the right of Jehovah's Witnesses to refuse blood transfusions, on the grounds that they consider them sinful, but some argue that the case of a pregnant woman is different because the life of an unborn child is at stake. Robert Orr of the Loma Linda University Center for Christian Bioethics acknowledged that physicians have a duty to explore alternatives to blood transfusions—an entire field of "bloodless medicine" has developed in large part to accommodate the religious beliefs of Jehovah's Witnesses—but wrote, "If the alternative demanded is not a reasonable medical option, and by following it the

FROM THE BENCH

Can Parents Make Martyrs of Unborn Children?

In 1986, a court in the District of Columbia ordered doctors to perform a C-section on Ayesha Madyun, who had refused the procedure in part because she believed that her religion required that she make that decision and in part because she did not believe that the procedure was necessary. Four years later, in another case, an appeals court overruled the *Madyun* court's holding.

> The Court had before it parents who, in part, refused a Caesarean section on the basis of religious beliefs. Although both parents impressed the Court as sincere, it was evident that the stronger basis for their individual decisions was the belief that the surgical procedure was not necessary and that additional steps could be taken to enhance the possibility of a vaginal delivery. Neither parent, however, is a trained physician. To ignore the undisputed opinion of a skilled and trained physician to indulge the desires of the parents where, as here, there is a substantial risk to the unborn infant, is something the Court cannot do. Indeed, even if the religious beliefs of the parents were the primary or sole reason for refusing a Caesarean, the state had a compelling interest in ensuring this infant could be born. Parents may be free to become martyrs themselves. But it does not follow they are free, in identical circumstances, to make martyrs of their children before they have reached the age of full and legal discretion when they can make that choice for themselves. On these facts, the parents may not make a martyr of their unborn infant.

Source: *In re: Madyun*, 114 Daily Wash. L. Rptr. 2233 (D.C. Super. Ct. July 26, 1986) (citations and footnotes omitted), *reversed, In re: A.C.,* 573 A.2d 1235 (D.C. App. 1990).

[unborn child] would be doomed, it may be justified to override the refusal." [178]

Pro-life advocates also defend the criminal prosecution of women whose refusal to have a C-section leads to the stillbirth of a child. Although critics of Rowland's prosecution complained that she was being charged with a crime because of a personal choice she had made, Jennifer Graham pointed out, "[Our] whole criminal justice system is based on prosecuting people because we don't like the choices they make." [179] Joseph Giganti of the American Life League wrote in an article that Rowland's actions were similar to the murder of Laci Peterson and her unborn son Conner, commenting, "innocent lives were needlessly ended. As part of a society that considers itself moral and just, the proper authorities are seeking the legal redress to these murders, as is their duty." [180]

Some pro-life advocates do not dispute pro-choice claims that obtaining court orders that require women to undergo C-sections undermines the legal right to choose an abortion. Rather, they say, cases such as Melissa Rowland's should raise awareness of the importance of protecting unborn children. Noting that pro-choice advocates worry "that the long hibernating moral conscience of American society might be roused by such sterling examples of the callous disregard for human life that the abortion industry has fostered in our society," Giganti wrote, "I hope they are right." [181]

In cases of mental incompetence, a guardian can protect the rights of an unborn child.

Actions such as prosecuting women for substance abuse during pregnancy and ordering pregnant women to undergo medical procedure are designed to protect unborn children from their mothers' bad decisions. Critics of such actions argue that women should have the right to make their own decisions. One group of women does not have the legal right to make their own decisions: those who have court-appointed guardians because of unconsciousness, mental retardation, or mental illness. Such women are considered legally incompetent, or unable to make important decisions; therefore, courts appoint a legal guardian who is entitled to make decisions on behalf of the incompetent person, often called a "ward."

If a woman who is considered legally incompetent becomes pregnant, a court-appointed guardian has many important decisions to consider, including the decision whether she should have an abortion. That guardian is not bound in any way to consider the interests of the unborn child. Pro-life advocates argue that the unborn child's rights are completely ignored under traditional guardianship laws and therefore courts should appoint a separate guardian to represent the unborn child.

Although trial judges sometimes appoint guardians to represent unborn children, pro-life advocates have generally been frustrated by appeals court decisions. In a 2004 Florida case, *In re: J.D.S.*, a state appeals court ruled that Florida's guardianship law does not allow the appointment of a guardian for an unborn child. Judge Robert Pleus dissented, insisting that the phrase "minor under the age of 18"[182] in Florida's guardianship law is broad enough to cover a fetus. Displeased with the court's decision, he urged in his dissent that the legislature pass a new law to allow for the appointment of a guardian for an unborn child.

Pleus argued that the current law, as interpreted by the court, left the unborn child with nobody to advocate for his or her interests. A pregnant woman who is capable of making rational decisions usually makes decisions that take her unborn child's interests into account. In contrast, Pleus noted, the guardianship law does not permit the guardian to weigh the unborn child's interests:

> [Florida law] creates a "fiduciary" relationship between the ward and the guardian by requiring that in the management of the guardianship, the guardian be independent and impartial. The guardian of the mother owes a complete non-compromising

fiduciary relationship to the mother and the guardian is prohibited from compromising his or her duties owed to the ward by taking actions on behalf of the unborn child. This means the court-appointed guardian is placed in a "dilemma" when issues of the ward conflict with the welfare or health of the unborn child.[183]

A pregnant woman's guardian must make many medical decisions that affect both the woman and her unborn child. As a result of the guardian's uncompromising duty to the pregnant woman, Pleus wrote, the guardian is bound to make decisions that pose harm to the unborn child:

> Without a guardian for the baby, the court places the baby at the mercy of the decisions made by the court-appointed guardian. The record in this case, for example, indicates that J.D.S. is taking psychotropic medications which may jeopardize the welfare of the baby. In addition, future medical procedures such as tests and medication will be required which may detrimentally affect the baby's welfare. Matters such as whether to obtain a sonogram, use of anesthesia for medical procedures, the type of vitamins, choice of delivery, medications or other prenatal "dilemmas" will have a profound impact on the well-being of the unborn child. These issues alone create a conflict of interest that a court-appointed guardian over J.D.S. may not be able to resolve, inasmuch as the guardian owes a primary duty to J.D.S. and not to the baby. Hence, the guardian of J.D.S. is placed in an obvious conflict of interest which must be avoided.[184]

The dissenting opinion also expressed concern about abortion decisions made by guardians. Although the guardian appointed to represent J.D.S. did not choose for her to have an abortion, Pleus noted that, in another case that involved a mentally incompetent woman who was raped, the guardian did opt for abortion. Although the guardian had to seek the court's permission to authorize the abortion, Pleus wrote, "No guardian was there to advocate the interests of the unborn child."[185]

> • **Should the "right to choose" include a legal guardian's right to choose an abortion for another person?**

Judge Pleus added a personal touch to his opinion by writing about his grandson, who recently had been born. He mentioned how, on an ultrasound machine, he could watch his grandson move his arms and legs 14 weeks after conception. Pleus argued that his grandson was a person from the moment of conception and that the time has come for laws to recognize that life begins at conception. He concluded:

> We now know the baby of J.D.S. is a girl. She is called Baby S. She was born through Caesarean section. Ironically, within a short time after her birth, a guardian was appointed for Baby S. It makes no sense to me that Baby S could have a guardian after the Caesarean but not before. Was Baby S any less human before the surgery?[186]

Summary

Shocking cases of neglect have led pro-life advocates to argue that unborn children sometimes need protection from their mothers. Some support prosecution of women who use drugs during pregnancy, and others support court-ordered medical treatment, such as surgeries and blood transfusions, if they are needed to protect the life of an unborn child. One possible legal vehicle suggested is to appoint a legal guardian who can advocate for the unborn child's interests.

The Rise of Fetal Rights and Its Impact on Bioethics and the Abortion Debate

Passionate voices speak loudly on both sides of the fetal rights debate, with some arguing for expansive rights for unborn children and others arguing that a pregnant woman should have complete control over her embryo or fetus, without government interference. Public opinion on issues of fetal rights does not mirror public opinion on abortion rights. Many more people support laws like UVVA than support strict restrictions on abortion. To that extent, the pro-life movement has made inroads in the fetal rights debate that it has not been able to make in the abortion debate.

On the other hand, the pro-life movement has not had the same impact in the area of embryonic stem cell research. Embryonic stem cell research involves studying human cells that scientists can reproduce in a laboratory. The catch—and the concerns to many pro-life advocates—is that human embryos must be destroyed in order to get the original stem cell from which the copies are made. Even some opponents of abortion have spoken in favor of embryonic stem cell research, and the debate is hotly contested.

Fetal personhood and medical research.

Advocates of embryonic stem cell research maintain that the research holds the promise of finding cures for many terrible diseases. Scientists originally make embryonic stem cells by removing cells from a human embryo, typically one that was created in a laboratory with sperm and egg cells provided by a couple trying to conceive a baby through in vitro fertilization (IVF) and then frozen for later use. Fertility clinics typically produce more embryos during the process than the couple needs in order to have their desired number of children, and some couples donate their embryos for scientific research.

> • **Do you believe that it is acceptable for people to donate frozen embryos for medical research?**

Scientists can extract cells from these embryos—at a very early stage of development—to produce stem cells, which they can then replicate to produce a large supply of cells. The process of extracting the cells destroys the embryo, but afterward, no further embryos are destroyed and the stem cells created in the laboratory are—unlike a fertilized egg—incapable of developing into a living human. Because the four or eight cells of an early embryo must develop into brain cells, heart cells, kidney cells, and so forth, however, the stem cells are capable of producing a wide variety of human tissues and organs. This potential to produce a variety of tissues and organs, some believe, makes stem cell research a potential source of cures for Alzheimer's disease, Lou Gehrig's disease, paralysis, cancer, and other conditions that people speculate could be cured with a supply of human tissues or cells.

Pro-life organizations oppose stem cell research because it involves destruction of a human embryo. Richard Doerflinger, deputy director of the United States Conference of Catholic Bishops, summarized the Catholic Church's position on stem cell research in testimony before Congress:

> Every human life, from the first moment of existence until natural death, deserves our respect and protection. . . . Thus Catholic morality regarding respect for human life, and any secular ethic in agreement with its basic premises, rejects all deliberate involvement with the direct killing of human embryos for research or any other purpose. Such killing is gravely and intrinsically wrong, and no promised beneficial consequences can lessen that wrong.[187]

Noted French geneticist Jerome Lejeune has referred to frozen embryos as being trapped in a "concentration can," similar to Nazi concentration camps in which Jews and others were imprisoned, subjected to cruel experiments, and murdered. He wrote that frozen embryos are "not spare parts which we could take at random, they are not experimental material that we could throw away after using it, they are not commodities that we could exchange . . ."[188]

On August 9, 2001, the Bush administration dealt a blow to embryonic stem cell research by announcing that federal funding would be available only for research on stem cells derived from embryos destroyed before that date. Research on stem cells derived from embryos destroyed after that date would have to be funded other means, such as by states, universities, or private donors. In November 2004, California voters approved a ballot measure that authorized the state to issue bonds to fund embryonic stem cell research in the state.

The Bush administration's rationale for its decision was that it did not want to encourage the future destruction of human embryos, but the embryos used to create the then existing "cell lines" had already been destroyed. Many have questioned the administration's policy. Opponents of embryonic stem cell research believe that the administration's "the damage is already done" approach wrongly rewards the earlier destruction of human life. Proponents argue that the cell lines already in existence do not provide scientists with enough variety to develop and study human tissue. Concerns increased after scientists announced that some of the existing cell lines had been contaminated and could not be used for further study. Harvard Medical School Professor George Daley testified to Congress:

> In the three years since the President announced his policy, over a hundred additional lines have been generated, many with advantageous properties that make them highly valuable to medical scientists. Some of these new lines model diseases like cystic fibrosis, muscular dystrophy, and genetic forms of mental retardation. What does the President say to families whose children are affected by these devastating diseases?[189]

Although embryonic stem cell research remained legal, supporters of embryonic stem cell research fear that fetal rights laws threaten the continued legality of stem cell research. Democratic Senator Dianne Feinstein of California, when opposing the passage of UVVA, argued:

> [UVVA supporters'] agenda [is] freezing the law, any law, in this case criminal law, that life begins at conception. Then, once declared legally, that law becomes the stepping-stone to refuse embryonic stem cell research. . . . Once the law defines human life as beginning at conception, stem cell research could become murder. . . .
>
> Everyone in this body who believes embryonic stem cell research holds a promise for cures to Parkinson's, for cures to Alzheimer's, for cures to juvenile diabetes, for perhaps spinal cord rupture repair, will have to contend with a statute that has said life begins at conception. So embryonic stem cell research may become murder. . . .[190]

UVVA does not apply to stem cell research because the law protects only unborn children developing in a woman's uterus, not embryos stored in a laboratory. As Feinstein predicted, however, pro-life groups have seized on fetal rights measures, such as UVVA and the Bush administration's decision to cover unborn children under the State Children's Health Insurance Program (SCHIP), to argue in favor of a ban on embryonic stem cell research. In his Congressional testimony, less than six months after the passage of UVVA, Doerflinger noted:

THE LETTER OF THE LAW

California Ponders Funding Stem Cell Research With State Funds

Because the Bush administration's policy limited federal funding of embryonic stem cell research, researchers began to look for new sources of funding. In California, proponents of embryonic stem cell research gathered support for a ballot initiative in which the voters had the opportunity to adopt a law without the involvement of the state's legislature. The initiative, which passed in November 2004, authorized 3 billion dollars to support research within the state.

The people of California find and declare the following:

Millions of children and adults suffer from devastating diseases or injury that are currently incurable, including Cancer, Diabetes, Heart Disease, Alzheimer's, Parkinson's, Spinal Cord injuries, Blindness, Lou Gehrig's Disease, HIV/AIDS, Mental Health disorders, Multiple Sclerosis, Huntington's Disease and more than 70 other diseases and injuries.

Recently medical science has discovered a new way to attack chronic diseases and injuries. The cure and treatment of these diseases can potentially be accomplished through the use of new regenerative medical therapies including a special type of human cells, called stem cells. These life-saving medical breakthroughs can only happen if adequate funding is made available to advance stem cell research, develop therapies, and conduct clinical trials.

The principle that the embryo deserves recognition and respect as a member of the human family is also already reflected in numerous areas of federal law. At every stage of development, the unborn child in the womb is protected by federal homicide laws as a separate victim when there is a violent attack upon his or her mother. That same child is recognized in federal health regulations as an eligible patient deserving prenatal care.[191]

About half of California's families have a child or adult who has suffered or will suffer from a serious, often critical or terminal medical condition that could potentially be treated or cured with stem cell therapies. In these cases of chronic illness or when patients face a medical crisis, the healthcare system may simply not be able to meet the needs of patients or control spiraling costs unless therapy focus switches away from maintenance and toward prevention and cures.

Unfortunately, the federal government is not providing adequate funding necessary for the urgent research and facilities needed to develop stem cell therapies to treat and cure diseases and serious injuries. This critical funding gap currently prevents the rapid advancement of research that could benefit millions of Californians.

The California Stem Cell Research and Cures Act will close this funding gap by establishing an Institute which will issue bonds to support stem cell research, emphasizing pluripotent stem cell and progenitor cell research and other vital medical technologies, for the development of life-saving regenerative medical treatments and cures.

Source: The California Stem Cell and Cures Initiative, Prop. 71 (November 2, 2004).

Doerflinger also argued that recognition of a human embryo as a "person" was not critical to the opposition of embryonic stem cell research. He testified:

> [People] who do not hold the human embryo to be a full-fledged human person can conclude that embryonic stem cell research is unethical. Many moral wrongs fall short of the full gravity of homicide but are nonetheless seriously wrong. Setting aside "personhood," surely no one prefers funding research that requires destroying human life.[192]

Despite Doerflinger's assertion, many people do not consider embryonic stem cell research, which requires destroying an embryo with just a few cells, to be "destroying human life." Even people who do not have a moral objection to stem cell research might object to research on human embryos at later stages of development, however. Rather than extracting the cells from an early-stage embryo, scientists can allow the embryo to continue to grow in the laboratory and then conduct research on a developing human. As with embryonic stem cells, scientists hope that research on more mature embryos also will lead to medical breakthroughs. Many people oppose use of human embryos as subjects of medical research, because the embryos are destroyed in the process. The question of when personhood begins, discussed in previous chapters, is clearly relevant to the debate over embryo research. Even some people who support abortion rights are uneasy with the idea of "farming" humans for research purposes.

The President's Council on Bioethics recommended to Congress that it "prohibit the use of human embryos in research beyond a designated stage in their development (between 10 and 14 days after fertilization),"[193] as well as ban the transfer of a human embryo into an animal's uterus—or a woman's uterus—for any purpose other than giving birth to a baby. Council member Daniel W. Foster and several others noted in a statement appended to the report that noted that "regulations such as these will not fully satisfy the objections of those who oppose stem cell research on the grounds that blastocysts are morally equivalent to babies."[194] They suggested, however, that the regulations did address the concerns of those who fear that scientists "might seek to transfer embryos into a women's uterus, or even a pig's uterus, to grow organs for transplant, creating the nightmare prospect of embryo farms, fetuses exploited for spare parts, and the commercialization of human life."[195]

> • **Is there a difference in the value of life of an embryo inside a woman's womb and an embryo frozen in the laboratory? Should the law treat the two differently?**

Some pro-life council members expressed the opinion that all embryo research—regardless of possible benefit—is, like "organ farming," morally unjustifiable. They recognized that establishing some time limits is better than nothing and represents a step toward a total ban on embryo research. Robert P. George and Alfonso Gomez-Lobo wrote:

> [We] favor protecting human life from the very beginning by banning the use of living human embryos at any stage of development as disposable research material. Until this becomes politically feasible, we support efforts to accord as much protection as possible by limiting the number of days beyond which the law tolerates deliberate embryo killing. . . .
>
> It is our hope that citizens who share our fundamental commitment to the principle of the full and equal dignity of every member of the human family will join us in endorsing the Council's unanimous recommendation to Congress to establish a limit on embryo-destructive research. We pledge to join with them in working to establish yet more complete protection for human life in all stages and conditions.[196]

Other council members urged Congress not to go too far in regulating human embryo research. Michael Gazzaniga acknowledged that some people have a religious belief that a human embryo is a person but rejected the suggestion that this belief—as many assert—is based on scientific fact. He wrote:

> At the center of the discussion is the belief on the part of some that a blastocyst, the entity in the Petri dish, is morally equivalent to a living post-natal human being. For those who simply assert that equivalence, no matter what the scientific data might be, there is nothing more to be said. But for those who think the equivalence is due to "scientific fact" there is hope they may come to a deeper understanding of the nature of the problem.[197]

Gazzaniga expressed his support for biomedical cloning—"copying" embryos in a laboratory for research purposes, arguing that without the environment of a woman's uterus within which to grow, an embryo is not a person. He wrote, "Looking at a minuscule ball of cells in a Petri dish, so small that it could rest on the head of a pin, finds one hard pressed to think of it as a human being. After all, it has no brain or capacity to think and feel. . . . It is the dynamics between genes and environment that make a human being." [198]

- **Is it possible to set a time at which experimenting on a human embryo becomes unacceptable?**

Will fetal rights laws undermine *Roe* v. *Wade*?

People on both sides of the abortion debate made emotional comments when UVVA became law. Kim Gandy of NOW, referring to the law's definition of a person as including a member of the species *Homo sapiens* at any stage of development, direly predicted, "Such a definition of 'person' could entitle fertilized eggs, embryos and fetuses to legal rights—ultimately, setting the stage to legally reverse *Roe* [v. *Wade*]." [199] Tony Perkins of the pro-life Family Research Council declared, "Today marks a tremendous victory for the pro-life movement. We are now one giant step closer to rebuilding a culture of life, where every child—born and unborn—is given the protections they so clearly deserve."[200]

Despite the poignancy of these remarks, few believe that the current nine justices of the Supreme Court would use the legal definition of personhood contained in UVVA as a rationale for overturning *Roe* v. *Wade*. In past cases, the Supreme Court has visited the issue on several occasions, and each time, relatively conservative Justice Sandra Day O'Connor has been the "swing vote." Although she has generally sided with the more conservative justices in approving restrictions on abortion, she has joined the liberal justices in voting not to overturn *Roe* v. *Wade*.

Major changes in the makeup of the Supreme Court are likely on the horizon, and the outcome of the 2004 presidential election will play a big role in determining what those changes will look like. The president nominates candidates for the Supreme Court, and the Senate votes to affirm or deny the lifetime position. Writing before the 2004 presidential election, former Nixon White House lawyer John Dean predicted that the winner could appoint up to three justices, with O'Connor, John Paul Stevens (a supporter of *Roe* v. *Wade*), and Chief Justice William Rehnquist (an opponent of *Roe* v. *Wade*) all likely to retire soon. Dean predicted that the Senate confirmation process to replace the justices would be contentious: "Given the importance to the bases of both parties, a major battle is brewing for these seats. It is not going to be pretty."[201]

Soon after George W. Bush's victory, the public learned that Chief Justice Rehnquist was undergoing treatment for thyroid cancer. This revelation further fueled speculation that the president soon would appoint new Supreme Court justices. Republican Senator Arlen Specter of Pennsylvania, one of the few prominent pro-choice Republicans in Congress, warned that appointing a justice who would overturn *Roe* v. *Wade* would not be easy and promised to use his role on the Senate Judiciary

Committee to block nominations of stridently pro-life judges. After a backlash from fellow Republicans, Specter retreated somewhat from his comments, but most political observers agree with Dean's prediction that Senate battles over Supreme Court nominations could become very ugly.

In a Supreme Court with conservative justices in the majority, the types of laws discussed in this book—laws that define embryos as people, laws that recognize embryos as murder victims, and court decisions that regulate the conduct of pregnant women—serve as a potential basis for the Court to revisit a central holding of *Roe* v. *Wade*: that an embryo or fetus does not fit within the meaning of "person" under the Fourteenth Amendment to the U.S. Constitution, which requires states to protect life, liberty, and property. Although supporters of fetal rights laws have, for the most part, denied that they are trying to influence the abortion debate, many are suspicious of their motives. When UVVA became law, *Boston Globe* columnist Cathy Young noted, "Today, the bill's pro-life supporters may assert that it will not affect abortion rights; in the future, they may well use its logic to advocate a ban on abortion, arguing that it's absurd to make the personhood of the fetus contingent on whether the woman wants to go through with the pregnancy." [202]

• **Are pro-choice advocates taking too extreme a position by opposing laws like "Laci and Conner's Law?"**

Sensing a turn in the tides, Young suggested that it might be time for abortion rights supporters to take a more moderate stand on fetal rights. She noted that pro-choice advocates' opposition to UVVA made them appear to be "callous" and "extreme ideological zealots." [203] She suggested that, rather than staunchly opposing the recognition that a fetus could be a crime victim distinct from a pregnant woman, pro-choice advocates could have supported a bill that recognizes viable fetuses as murder victims while providing enhanced penalties for crimes against a woman carrying a previable embryo or fetus. Such a compromise law would have been less likely to threaten the right to choose an abortion before viability. Young cautioned pro-life advocates that "extremism" on the fetal rights issue might be "a ticket to defeat" on the abortion issue.[204]

Summary

The legal debate over fetal rights (or the rights of unborn children) comes at a critical juncture in American legal history. As the state legislatures and the U.S. Congress examine questions such as fetal homicide and definitions of personhood, their decisions have great potential to affect other critical areas of the law. Major changes in the composition of the U.S. Supreme Court are likely, and fetal rights laws could affect the court's reconsideration of the right to choose an abortion. In addition, embryonic stem cell research remains controversial, and Congress and the presidential administration might very well be influenced by the fetal rights debate in determining whether human embryos can be used for medical research.

Introduction

1. *In re: Guardianship of J.D.S.*, No. 5D03-1921 (5th Dist. Fla., Jan. 9, 2004) (Pleus, J., dissenting).

2. Johannes L. Jacobse, "Women Are Abortion's Second Victims." Review of *Forbidden Grief: The Unspoken Pain of Abortion* by Theresa Burke, Ph.D., and David Reardon, Ph.D. Available online at *www.orthodoxytoday.org/article-sprint/JacobseForbiddenGriefP.shtml*.

3. Rachel Roth, *Making Women Pay: The Hidden Cost of Fetal Rights*. Ithaca, NY: Cornell University Press, 2000, p. 92.

4. *Planned Parenthood of South Eastern Pa. v. Casey*, 505 U.S. 833 (1992).

5. Roth, *Making Women Pay*, p. 20.

6. Unborn Victims of Violence Act of 2004, Pub. L. No. 108-212, 108th Cong (2004).

Point: An Embryo or Fetus Does Not Deserve Legal Recognition as a Person

7. Catherine Whitney, *Whose Life? A Balanced Comprehensive View of Abortion from Its Historical Context to the Current Debate*. New York: William Morrow and Company, 1991, p. 119.

8. Andrea Mineo, "Beating the Odds." *Long Island Press*, July 3, 2003.

9. *Roe* v. *Wade*, 410 U.S. 113 (1973).

10. Ibid.

11. Joyce Arthur, "Personhood: Is a Fetus a Human Being?" August 2001. Available online at *http://mypage.direct.ca/w/writer/fetusperson.html*.

12. Vanessa Cullins, *Ask Dr. Cullins*, August 8, 2003. A publication of Planned Parenthood Foundation of America. Available online at *http://www.plannedparenthood.org/drcullins/030808_begin.asp*.

13. Robert H. Bork, *The Tempting of America: The Political Seduction of the Law*. New York: Touchstone, 1990, p. 112.

14. *Roe* v. *Wade*, 410 U.S. 113 (1973) (citations and footnotes omitted).

15. Barbara Duden, *Disembodying Women: Perspectives on Pregnancy and the Unborn*. Cambridge, MA: Harvard University Press, 1993, p. 59.

16. Lynn M. Morgan and Monica J. Casper to Centers for Medicare and Medicaid Services (April 9, 2002).

17. Janet Hadley, *Abortion: Between Freedom and Necessity*. Philadelphia: Temple University Press, 1996, p. 61.

18. Roth, *Making Women Pay*, p. 20.

19. National Abortion Rights Action League, Comments to the Proposed Change to the State Children's Health Insurance Program, U.S. Department of Health and Human Services, 67 C.F.R. sec. 9936, (March 5, 2002).

20. Ibid.

21. Planned Parenthood Foundation of America, *Nine Reasons Why Abortions Are Legal*, March, 1989. Available online at *http://www.plannedparenthood.org/ABORTION/9reasons.html*.

22. Lynn M. Morgan and Monica J. Casper, "Fetus Shouldn't Rob Woman of Personhood." *Springfield Sunday Republican*, May 2, 2004.

23. Ibid.

24. Roth, *Making Women Pay*, p. 91.

25. Hadley, *Abortion*, p. 61.

26. Ibid.

27. Arthur, "Personhood," *http://mypage.direct.ca/w/writer/fetusperson.html*.

28. Hadley, *Abortion*, p. 61.

29. Ibid.

30. National Organization for Women, Transcript of *Reframing Abortion Rights: Briefing on "Breaking the Abortion Deadlock, From Choice to Consent,"* January 21, 1997.

31. Ibid.

32. Donald P. Judges, *Hard Choices, Lost Voices: How the Abortion Debate Has Divided America, Distorted Constitutional Rights, and Damaged the Courts*. Chicago: Ivan R. Dee, 1993, p. 151.

33. Ibid.

34. Whitney, *Whose Life?*, p. 207.

35. *Davis* v. *Davis*, 842 S.W.2d 588, 597 (Tenn. 1992).

36. Ibid.

37. U.S. Department of Health and Human Services, Announcement of the Availability of Financial Assistance and Request for Applications to Support Development and Delivery of Public Awareness Campaigns on Embryo Adoption. Fed. Reg. 67 No. 143, (July 25, 2002).

38. Jeffrey Kahn, "'Adoption' of frozen embryos a loaded term," CNN.com, September 17, 2002. Available online at *http://www.cnn.com/2002/HEALTH/09/ 17/ethics.matters*.

39. Cong. Rec. S3137, (March 25, 2004.)

40. Rebecca Farmer, "'Fetal Rights' Initiatives Concern Abortion Rights Supporters," *National NOW Times*, Fall 2001. A publication of the National Organization for Women.

Counterpoint: An Unborn Child Is a Person Who Deserves Equal Protection Under the Law

41. Pope John Paul II, *Evangelium Vitae; On the Value and Inviolability of Human Life*. Washington, D.C.: U.S. Conference of Catholic Bishops, 1995, chap. 2, sec. 44.

42. Sacred Congregation for the Doctrine of the Faith, *The Gift of Life (Donum Vitae): Instruction on Respect for Human Life In its Origin and the Dignity of Procreation: Replies to Certain Questions of the Day*. Washington, D.C.: U.S. Conference of Catholic Bishops, 1987, pt. 1, sec. 1.

43. Ibid.

44. John Allen, "Under Vatican Ruling, Abortion Triggers Automatic Excommunication," *National Catholic Reporter*, January 17, 2003.

45. Sacred Congregation for the Doctrine of the Faith, *The Gift of Life*, pt. 1, sec. 1.

46. Francis J. Beckwith, "Abortion, Bioethics and Personhood: A Philosophical Reflection," *The Center for Bioethics and Human Dignity Commentary*, November 19, 2001. Available online at *http://www.cbhd.org/ resources/bioethics/beckwith_2001-11-19 .htm*.

47. Eugene Hoyas, "A Brief, Air-Tight Argument Against Abortion." 48 NEW OXFORD REV (2001). Available online at *http://www.newoxfordreview.org/2001/ sep01/eugenehoyas.html*.

48. Ibid.

49. Ibid.

50. Ibid.

51. Beckwith, "Abortion, Bioethics, and Personhood," *http://www.cbhd.org/ resources/bioethics/beckwith_2001- 11-19_print.htm*.

52. Ibid.

53. Keith A. Fournier and William Watkins, *In Defense of Life: Taking a Stand Against the Culture of Death*. Colorado Springs: NavPress, 1996, p. 30.

54. Mary Meehan, "ACLU v. Unborn Children." HUMAN LIFE REV (2001). Available online at *http://www.humanlifereview .com/2001_spring/meehan_s2001.php*.

55. Sacred Congregation for the Doctrine of the Faith, *The Gift of Life*, pt. 1, sec. 1.

56. *Dred Scott* v. *Sandford*, 60 U.S. 393 (1857).

57. "Sanctity of Human Life," Cong Rec H9366, 108th Cong. (October 8, 2003).

58. U.S. Constitution, Amendment XIV.

59. *Roe* v. *Wade*, 410 U.S. 113 (1973).

60. Beckwith, "Abortion, Bioethics, and Personhood."

61. *Akron* v. *Akron Center for Reproductive Health, Inc.*, 462 U.S. 416 (1983).

62. Mo. Rev. Stat. 1.205.1(1), (2), cited in *Webster* v. *Reproductive Health Services*, 492 U.S. 490 (1989).

63. *Aka* v. *Jefferson Hospital Association*, 42 SW.3d 508 (Ark. 2001), citing Ark. Const. amend. 68, § 2.

64. Ibid., citing Ark. Code Ann. § 5-1-102(13)(B)(i).

65. Ibid.

66. 42 C.F.R. sec. 457.10.

67. Pub. L. No. 108-212, 108th Cong. (2004).

68. John Walker, *Abortion and the Question of the Person.* Wheaton, MD: Libertarians for Life, undated.

69. *Webster* v. *Reproductive Health Services,* 492 U.S. 490 (1989) (Opinion of Rehnquist, C.J.).

70. Brief for Amicus Curiae Knights of Columbus, *Webster v. Reproductive Health Services,* 492 U.S. 490 (1989). Cited in Barbara Hinkson Craig and David M. O'Brien, *Abortion and American Politics.* Chatham, NJ: Chatham House Publishers, 1993, p. 210.

71. *Commonwealth* v. *Morris,* No. 2002-SC-0845-DG (Ky., June 17, 2004) (Wintersheimer, J., concurring).

Point: Fetal Homicide Laws Threaten Women's Rights

72. *Unborn Victims of Violence Act: Hearing Before the House Subcommittee on the Constitution,* 108th Cong. (2003).

73. Callie M. Rennison, *Intimate Partner Violence, 1993–2001* (February 2003). A publication of the U.S. Bureau of Justice Statistics.

74. Patricia Tjaden and Nancy Thoennes, *Extent, Nature, and Consequences of Intimate Partner Violence.* Washington, D.C.: National Institute of Justice and the Centers for Disease Control and Prevention, 2000.

75. Ibid.

76. Committee on the Judiciary, U.S. House of Representatives. *Report on Laci and Conner's Law.* 108th Congress, 2d Session, Report 108-420 (February 11, 2004) (dissenting view).

77. Ibid.

78. Ibid.

79. Ibid.

80. Ibid. (citing Amendment to H.R. 1997, 108th Congress, 2d Session).

81. Ibid. (remarks of Rep. Lofgren).

82. Ibid.

83. Pub. L. No. 108-212, 108th Cong. (2004).

84. National Abortion Rights Action League, press release, *Statement of President Kate Michelman on "Unborn Victims of Violence Act,"* February 26, 2004.

85. Ibid.

86. Michael C. Dorf, "How Abortion Politics Impedes Clear Thinking on Other Issues Involving Fetuses," *FindLaw's Writ,* May 28, 2003. Available online at http://writ.findlaw.com/commentary/20030528.html.

87. National Organization for Women, press release, *Bush's Latest Masquerade Exposed as Attack on Women's Reproductive Health,* April 1, 2004.

88. *Roe* v. *Wade,* 410 U.S. 113 (1973).

89. Dorf, "Abortion Politics."

90. Ibid.

91. *State* v. *MacGuire,* 84 P.3d 1171 (Utah 2004) (citing Utah Code Section 76-5-201(1)).

92. Ibid. (citing Utah Code Section 76-5-202(1)(b))

93. Ibid. (Durham, C.J. dissenting).

94. Alec Walen, "If *Roe v. Wade* Is Overruled, What Arguments Should Abortion Rights Supporters Use?" *FindLaw's Writ,* February 18, 2003. Available online at *http://writ.findlaw.com/commentary/20030218_walen.html.*

95. Ibid.

96. Unborn Victims of Violence Act of 2004, Pub. L. No. 108-212, 108th Cong (2004).

97. Cong. Rec. H647 (February 26, 2004).

98. Ibid.

99. Ibid.

Counterpoint: Laws Must Protect Every Unborn Child From Violence

100. House Subcommittee, *Unborn Victims of Violence Act.*

101. Ibid.

102. Cong. Rec. 3137 (March 25, 2004).

103. Ibid.

104. House Subcommittee, *Unborn Victims of Violence Act.*

105. Ibid.

106. Ibid.

107. Ibid.

108. Ibid.

109. Ibid.

110. Sharon Rocha to Hon. John Kerry, July 7, 2003. Made available by National Right to Life Committee.

111. President George W. Bush, *Signing Statement, Unborn Victims of Violence Act of 2004,* April 1, 2004.

112. Ibid.

113. House Subcommittee, *Unborn Victims of Violence Act.*

114. House Committee, *Report on Laci and Conner's Law.*

115. House Subcommittee, *Unborn Victims of Violence Act.*

116. Maggie Gallagher, "The Real John Kerry Stands up," *townhall.com,* April 1, 2004. Available online at *http://www.townhall. com/columnists/maggiegallagher/printmg 20040401.shtml.*

117. Jay Sekulow, "Murder of an Unborn Child and the Abortion Debate—Jay Explains." Available on line at *http:// www.aclj.org/news/Read.aspx?ID=540.*

118. Ibid.

119. House Subcommittee, *Unborn Victims of Violence Act.*

120. Ibid.

121. Ibid.

122. Unborn Victims of Violence Act of 2004, Pub. L. No. 108-212, 108th Cong.

123. *Commonwealth v. Morris,* No. 2002-SC-0845-DG (Ky., June 17, 2004) (Wintersheimer, J., concurring).

124. Ibid.

Point: Laws That Regulate the Conduct of Pregnant Women Invade Their Privacy

125. *In re A.C.,* 573 A.2d 1235 (D.C. App. 1990) (en banc).

126. Ibid.

127. *Whitner v. State,* 492 S.E.2d 777 (S.C. 1997).

128. *Ferguson v. City of Charleston.* 532 U.S. 67 (2001).

129. *State v. McKnight,* 577 S.E.2d 456 (S.C. 2003).

130. Brief for Amicus Curiae South Carolina State NOW, *State v. McKnight,* 577 S.E.2d 456 (S.C. 2003).

131. Roth, *Making Women Pay,* pp. 146–47.

132. Lynn M. Paltrow, "Pregnant Drug Users, Fetal Persons, and the Threat to *Roe v. Wade.*" 62 ALB. L. REV. (1999), p. 1024.

133. Cynthia Daniels, *At Women's Expense: State Power and the Politics of Fetal Rights.* Cambridge, MA: Harvard University Press, 1993, p. 116.

134. Paltrow, "Pregnant Drug Users," p. 1020.

135. Brief for Amicus Curiae South Carolina Medical Association, *State v. McKnight,* 577 S.E.2d 456 (S.C. 2003), citing T. A. Slotkin, "Fetal Nicotine or Cocaine Exposure: Which One is Worse?" *285 J. Pharmacology & Experimental Therapeutics 931* (1998).

136. Roth, *Making Women Pay,* p. 147.

137. SCMA Brief.

138. Brief for Amici Curiae American Public Health Association et al., *People v. Gilligan,* No. 2003-1192 (Glen Falls, NY, 2003).

139. SCMA Brief.

140. SCMA Brief.

141. Paltrow, "Pregnant Drug Users," p. 1051.

142. Ibid.

143. *Cruzan v. Director, Missouri Department of Health,* 497 U.S. 261 (1990).

144. David Weiss, "Court Delivers Controversy," *Wilkes-Barre (Pa.) Times-Leader,* January 16, 2004.

145. *In re Brown,* 689 N.E.2d 397 (Ill. App., 1997).

146. American College of Obstetricians and Gynecologists, *Ethics in Obstetrics and Gynecology.* Washington, D.C.: ACOG, 2004, p. 34.

147. Ibid., p. 36.

148. Roth, *Making Women Pay*, p. 90.

149. Daniels, *At Women's Expense*, p. 41.

150. Ibid., p. 40.

151. Roth, *Making Women Pay*, p. 91.

152. Robert G. Costello, "Fetal Endangerment: A Challenge for Criminal Law." 4 CAL. CRIMINAL JUSTICE REV. June 2001.

153. ACLU brief.

154. ACLU brief

155. ACLU brief.

156. *In re: Guardianship of J.D.S.*, No. 5D03-1921 (5th Dist. Fla., January 9, 2004).

Counterpoint: In Some Cases, the Law Must Protect Unborn Children From Their Mothers' Behavior

157. Jennifer Graham, "Give Me a 'C,'" *National Review Online,* March 16, 2004. Available online at *http://www.nationalreview.com/ jgraham/graham200403160901.asp.*

158. *State* v. *McKnight*, 576 S.E.2d 168 (S.C. 2003), cert. denied, *McKnight v. South Carolina*, 124 S. Ct. 101 (2003).

159. Quoted in Michael L. Betsch, "Conservatives Hail 'Landmark' Pro-Life Decision In SC," *CNSNews.com,* February 3, 2003.

160. National Clearinghouse on Alcohol and Drug Information, *Alcohol, Tobacco, and Other Drugs and Pregnancy and Parenthood.* Rockville, MD: NCADI, 1995, (footnotes omitted). Available online at *http://www.health.org/govpubs/ ml010/default.aspx.*

161. Brief for Respondent, *Ferguson* v. *City of Charleston*, 532 U.S. 67 (2001).

162. Charles M. Condon, "Clinton's Cocaine Babies: Why Won't the Administration Let Us Save Our Children?" POLICY REV. (1995). Available online at *http://www .policyreview.org/spring95/condth.html.*

163. Brief for Respondent, *Ferguson v. City of Charleston.*

164. Condon, "Clinton's Cocaine Babies."

165. Louise M. Chan, "S.O.S. from the Womb: A Call for New York Legislation Criminalizing Drug Use During Pregnancy," 21 FORDHAM URB. L.J. (1993) 199.

166. Paul A. Logli, "Save the Drug Babies," *The American Enterprise* (Law and Order Special Edition, May/June 1995). Available online at *http://www.taemag.com/ issues/articleid.16868/article_detail.asp.*

167. Ibid.

168. Condon, "Clinton's Cocaine Babies."

169. Logli, "Save the Drug Babies."

170. Condon, "Clinton's Cocaine Babies."

171. Ibid.

172. Quoted in Betsch, "Conservatives."

173. Scott B. Rae, "The Unkind Cut of Forced C-Sections," *Center for Bioethics and Human Dignity Commentary,* August 13, 2004. Available online at *http://www.cbhd.org/resources/reproductive/rae_2004-08-13.htm.*

174. Rae, "Unkind Cut," *http://www.cbhd.org/ resources/reproductive/rae_2004-08-13 .htm.*

175. Graham, "Give Me a 'C.'"

176. Ibid.

177. Rae, "Unkind Cut," *http://www.cbhd.org/ resources/reproductive/rae_2004-08-13 .htm.*

178. Robert Orr, "Clinical Ethics Consultation," 16 UPDATE (2000). Available at *http://www.llu.edu/llu/bioethics/ update161/orr.html.*

179. Graham, "Give Me a 'C.'"

180. Joseph R. Giganti, "Life Is Not Arbitrary; That's the Whole Point," *Washington Dispatch*, March 19, 2004.

181. Ibid.

182. *In re: Guardianship of J.D.S.*, No. 5D03-1921 (5th Dist. Fla., January 9, 2004) (Pleus, J., dissenting).

183. Ibid.

184. Ibid.

185. Ibid.

186. Ibid.

Conclusion

187. *Embryonic Stem Cell Research: Exploring the Controversy: Hearing before the Senate Subcommittee on Science, Technology, and Space,* 108th Cong. (2004).

188. Jerome Lejeune, *The Concentration Can: When Does Human Life Begin? An Eminent Geneticist Testifies.* San Francisco: Ignatius Press, 1992, p. 47.

189. Ibid.

190. Cong. Rec. S3127 (March 25, 2004).

191. House Subcommittee, *Embryonic Stem Cell Research.*

192. Ibid.

193. President's Commission on Bioethics, *Reproduction and Responsibility: The Regulation of New Biotechnologies.* Washington, D.C., March 2004, p. 223.

194. Ibid., p. 234.

195. Ibid.

196. Ibid., p. 244.

197. Ibid., p. 238.

198. Ibid.

199. National Organization for Women, press release, "Bush's Latest Masquerade Exposed as Attack on Women's Reproductive Health," April 1, 2004.

200. Family Research Council, press release, "FRC Praises Signing of 'Unborn Victims of Violence Act,'" April 1, 2004.

201. John Dean, "A Crucial But Largely Ignored 2004 Campaign Issue." *FindLaw's Writ,* September 24, 2004.

202. Cathy Young, "A Tough Loss for Left in Abortion War." *Boston Globe,* March 29, 2004.

203. Ibid.

204. Ibid.

Books and Reports

Craig, Barbara Hinkson, and David M. O'Brien. *Abortion and American Politics.* Chatham, NJ: Chatham House Publishers, 1993.

Daniels, Cynthia R. *At Women's Expense: State Power and the Politics of Fetal Rights.* Cambridge, MA: Harvard University Press, 1993.

Duden, Barbara. *Disembodying Women: Perspectives on Pregnancy and the Unborn.* Cambridge, MA: Harvard University Press, 1993.

Fournier, Keith A., and William Watkins. *In Defense of Life: Taking a Stand Against the Culture of Death.* Colorado Springs: NavPress, 1996.

Hadley, Janet. *Abortion: Between Freedom and Necessity.* Philadelphia: Temple University Press, 1996.

Judges, Donald P. *Hard Choices, Lost Voices: How the Abortion Debate Has Divided America, Distorted Constitutional Rights, and Damaged the Courts.* Chicago: Ivan R. Dee, 1993.

Lejeune, Jerome. *The Concentration Can: When Does Human Life Begin? An Eminent Geneticist Testifies.* San Francisco: Ignatius Press, 1992.

Pope John Paul II. *Evangelium Vitae: On the Value and Inviolability of Human Life.* Washington, D.C.: U.S. Conference of Catholic Bishops, 1995.

President's Commission on Bioethics. *Reproduction and Responsibility: The Regulation of New Bioetechnologies.* Washington, D.C.: 2004.

Roth, Rachel. *Making Women Pay: The Hidden Cost of Fetal Rights.* Ithaca, NY: Cornell University Press, 2000.

Sacred Congregation for the Doctrine of the Faith. *The Gift of Life (Donum Vitae): Instruction of Respect for Human Life in Its Origin and the Dignity of Procreation: Replies to Certain Questions of the Day.* Washington, D.C.: U.S. Conference of Catholic Bishops, 1987.

Whitney, Catherine. *Whose Life? A Balanced Comprehensive View of Abortion from Its Historical Context to the Current Debate.* New York: William Morrow and Company, 1991.

Websites

American College of Obstetricians and Gynecologists

http://www.acog.org

The American College of Obstetricians and Gynecologists (ACOG), which represents physicians who treat women and deliver babies, generally supports a woman's right to make her own health care and reproductive decisions over fetal rights. Individual members and special interest groups of obstetricians and gynecologists do support fetal rights.

American Life League

http://www.all.org

The American Life League, an independent Catholic organization, favors fetal rights and taking strong positions against abortion, birth control, and embryonic stem cell research. The organization's American Bioethics Advisory Committee offers numerous papers that support personhood beginning at conception.

Center for Bioethics and Human Dignity

http://www.cbhd.org

This conservative bioethics think tank generally supports fetal rights. It offers viewpoints on embryo adoption, forced C-sections, embryonic stem cell research, and the beginning of life.

Human Life Review

http://www.humanlifereview.com

This journal is about pro-life issues. Online archives include articles about the personhood of unborn children.

International Cesarean Awareness Network

http://www.ican-online.org/

This organization opposes involuntary C-sections and argues that C-sections should be performed only when medically necessary. It offers advice to pregnant women about how to avoid unnecessary C-sections.

NARAL Pro-Choice America

http://www.naral.org

This advocacy group takes its name from "Abortion Rights Action League." The Website offers a briefing paper in opposition to fetal rights.

National Advocates for Pregnant Women

http://advocatesforpregnantwomen.org/

This national organization advocates for the rights of pregnant women and against fetal rights. It opposes prosecution of pregnant women for drug use, forcing unwanted medical procedures on pregnant women, fetal homicide laws, and other laws that recognize an embryo or fetus as a person.

National Organization for Women

http://www.now.org
This national feminist organization is involved with many women's issues and generally supports women's autonomy to make decisions and opposes any fetal rights measures.

National Right-to-Life Committee

http://www.nrlc.org
This national pro-life organization has many state affiliates. The Website contains position statements and personal stories in support of personhood and unborn victim laws.

Planned Parenthood Federation of America

http://www.ppfa.org
Planned Parenthood is pro-choice advocacy group and association of nonprofit birth control and abortion providers. The group opposes the development of fetal rights on the basis of its threat to reproductive choice.

President's Commission on Bioethics

http://www.bioethics.gov
This commission advises the president of the United States on bioethical issues, including embryonic stem cell research and other research that involves embryos. Online archives include detailed reports on these issues.

U.S. Conference of Catholic Bishops

http://www.usccb.org
This national organization represents Catholic dioceses. The Website has extensive information about pro-life issues, including documents that express the Catholic Church's position on personhood and stem cell research.

Yes on 71

http://www.yeson71.com
This Website supports the California Stem Cell Research and Cures Initiative, a ballot initiative passed in November 2004 granting state funding for embryonic stem cell research. Contains information about stem cell research and personal stories of people with currently incurable conditions.

Cases and Legislation

Aka v. Jefferson Hospital Association, 42 S.W.3d 508 (Ark. 2001).
The Arkansas Supreme Court ruled that parents can bring a wrongful death action on behalf of a child who was stillborn because of alleged medical malpractice.

Akron v. Akron Center for Reproductive Health, Inc., 462 U.S. 416 (1983).
The U.S. Supreme Court ruled that states cannot ban abortion by redefining the beginning of life, a ruling later clarified in *Webster* v. *Reproductive Health Services.*

Commonwealth v. Morris, No. 2002-SC-0845-DG (Ky., June 17, 2004)
The Kentucky Supreme Court overturned a conviction for killing an unborn child in an automobile accident. Although Kentucky passed a fetal homicide law after the accident occurred, the court ruled that the laws in effect at the time of the accident did not recognize an unborn child as a homicide victim.

Davis v. Davis, 842 S.W. 2d 588 (Tenn. 1992).
The Tennessee Supreme Court ruled that frozen embryos created through in vitro fertilization are neither property nor full-fledged people.

Embryo Adoption Policy, Federal Register 67, No. 143 (July 25, 2002).
This policy established federal funding for the "adoption" of embryos. Critics say that the policy creates legal complications—such as how to determine the welfare of the embryo—not present in embryo "donations," which are generally considered transfers of property.

Ferguson v. City of Charleston, 532 U.S. 67 (2001).
The U.S. Supreme Court invalidated a program of involuntarily testing pregnant women suspected of drug use and turning over test results to police for prosecution.

In re: A.C., 573 A.2d 1235 (D.C. App. 1990) (en banc).
An appeals court in the District of Columbia ruled that judges cannot order a woman to submit to a cesarean section against her will.

In re: Brown, 689 N.E.2d 397 (Ill. App. 1997)
An Illinois appeals court ruled that a judge cannot order a Jehovah's Witness to undergo a blood transfusion for the benefit of an embryo or fetus.

In re: Guardianship of J.D.S., NO. 5D03-1921 (Fla. 5th D.C.A., January 9, 2004)
A Florida appeals court ruled that a state's guardianship law does not allow a court to appoint a guardian to represent an embryo or fetus.

Roe v. Wade, 410 U.S. 113 (1973)
The U.S. Supreme Court held that a woman has a constitutional right to choose an abortion, and that—based on legal history—an unborn child is not a "person" protected by the U.S. Constitution.

137

State Children's Health Insurance Program, U.S. Department of Health and Human Services, 67 C.F.R. sec. 9936 (2002).
This policy of George W. Bush administration recognizes that unborn children are eligible for health care under a program that Congress created to provide health care to low-income children.

***State* v. *MacGuire*,** 84 P.3d 1171 (Utah 2004)
The Utah Supreme Court ruled that the murder of a pregnant woman constitutes the murder of two persons. The dissenting chief justice argued that the state did not have the constitutional power to confer personhood on an embryo or fetus.

***State* v. *McKnight*,** 577 S.E.2d 456 (S.C. 2003)
The South Carolina Supreme Court upheld the homicide conviction of a woman whose stillborn baby tested positive for traces of cocaine.

Unborn Victims of Violence Act of 2004 ("Laci and Conner's Law"), Pub. L. No. 108-212, 108th Cong. (2004)
Under federal law, violently killing or harming an unborn child (an embryo or fetus from time of conception onward) is punishable as a separate murder or assault. This law has no impact on state prosecutions.

***Webster* v. *Reproductive Health Services*,** 492 U.S. 490 (1989)
The U.S. Supreme Court upheld a Missouri law that defined conception as the beginning of life.

***Whitner* v. *State*,** 328 S.C. 1, 492 S.E.2d 777 (1997), *cert. denied* 523 U.S. 1145 (1998)
The South Carolina Supreme Court upheld the criminal child neglect conviction of woman whose baby tested positive for traces of cocaine at birth. The U.S. Supreme Court refused to hear the woman's appeal.

Terms and Concepts

abortion

bioethics

born alive rule

caesarean section (C-section)

embryo

embryonic stem cell research

fetal homicide laws

fetus

guardian

in utero

in vitro

incompetence

life, liberty, and property

personhood

pro-choice

pro-life

right to choose

Roe v. Wade

stillbirth

unborn child

unborn victims law

viability

zygote

Beginning Legal Research

The goal of POINT/COUNTERPOINT is not only to provide the reader with an introduction to a controversial issue affecting society, but also to encourage the reader to explore the issue more fully. This appendix, then, is meant to serve as a guide to the reader in researching the current state of the law as well as exploring some of the public-policy arguments as to why existing laws should be changed or new laws are needed.

Like many types of research, legal research has become much faster and more accessible with the invention of the Internet. This appendix discusses some of the best starting points, but of course "surfing the Net" will uncover endless additional sources of information—some more reliable than others. Some important sources of law are not yet available on the Internet, but these can generally be found at the larger public and university libraries. Librarians usually are happy to point patrons in the right direction.

The most important source of law in the United States is the Constitution. Originally enacted in 1787, the Constitution outlines the structure of our federal government and sets limits on the types of laws that the federal government and state governments can pass. Through the centuries, a number of amendments have been added to or changed in the Constitution, most notably the first ten amendments, known collectively as the Bill of Rights, which guarantee important civil liberties. Each state also has its own constitution, many of which are similar to the U.S. Constitution. It is important to be familiar with the U.S. Constitution because so many of our laws are affected by its requirements. State constitutions often provide protections of individual rights that are even stronger than those set forth in the U.S. Constitution.

Within the guidelines of the U.S. Constitution, Congress—both the House of Representatives and the Senate—passes bills that are either vetoed or signed into law by the President. After the passage of the law, it becomes part of the United States Code, which is the official compilation of federal laws. The state legislatures use a similar process, in which bills become law when signed by the state's governor. Each state has its own official set of laws, some of which are published by the state and some of which are published by commercial publishers. The U.S. Code and the state codes are an important source of legal research; generally, legislators make efforts to make the language of the law as clear as possible.

However, reading the text of a federal or state law generally provides only part of the picture. In the American system of government, after the legislature passes laws and the executive (U.S. President or state governor) signs them, it is up to the judicial branch of the government, the court system, to interpret the laws and decide whether they violate any provision of the Constitution. At the state level, each state's supreme court has the ultimate authority in determining what a law means and whether or not it violates the state constitution. However, the federal courts—headed by the U.S. Supreme Court—can review state laws and court decisions to determine whether they violate federal laws or the U.S. Constitution. For example, a state court may find that a particular criminal law is valid under the state's constitution, but a federal court may then review the state court's decision and determine that the law is invalid under the U.S. Constitution.

It is important, then, to read court decisions when doing legal research. The Constitution uses language that is intentionally very general—for example, prohibiting "unreasonable searches and seizures" by the police—and court cases often provide more guidance. For example, the U.S. Supreme Court's 2001 decision in *Kyllo* v. *United States* held that scanning the outside of a person's house using a heat sensor to determine whether the person is growing marijuana is unreasonable—*if* it is done without a search warrant secured from a judge. Supreme Court decisions provide the most definitive explanation of the law of the land, and it is therefore important to include these in research. Often, when the Supreme Court has not decided a case on a particular issue, a decision by a federal appeals court or a state supreme court can provide guidance; but just as laws and constitutions can vary from state to state, so can federal courts be split on a particular interpretation of federal law or the U.S. Constitution. For example, federal appeals courts in Louisiana and California may reach opposite conclusions in similar cases.

Lawyers and courts refer to statutes and court decisions through a formal system of citations. Use of these citations reveals which court made the decision (or which legislature passed the statute) and when and enables the reader to locate the statute or court case quickly in a law library. For example, the legendary Supreme Court case *Brown* v. *Board of Education* has the legal citation 347 U.S. 483 (1954). At a law library, this 1954 decision can be found on page 483 of volume 347 of the U.S. Reports, the official collection of the Supreme Court's decisions. Citations can also be helpful in locating court cases on the Internet.

Understanding the current state of the law leads only to a partial under-standing of the issues covered by the POINT/COUNTERPOINT series. For a fuller understanding of the issues, it is necessary to look at public-policy arguments that the current state of the law is not adequately addressing the issue. Many groups lobby for new legislation or changes to existing legislation; the National Rifle Association (NRA), for example, lobbies Congress and the state legislatures constantly to make existing gun control laws less restrictive and not to pass additional laws. The NRA and other groups dedicated to various causes might also intervene in pending court cases: a group such as Planned Parenthood might file a brief *amicus curiae* (as "a friend of the court")—called an "amicus brief"—in a lawsuit that could affect abortion rights. Interest groups also use the media to influence public opinion, issuing press releases and frequently appearing in interviews on news programs and talk shows. The books in POINT/COUNTERPOINT list some of the interest groups that are active in the issue at hand, but in each case there are countless other groups working at the local, state, and national levels. It is important to read everything with a critical eye, for sometimes interest groups present information in a way that can be read only to their advantage. The informed reader must always look for bias.

Finding sources of legal information on the Internet is relatively simple thanks to "portal" sites such as FindLaw (*www.findlaw.com*), which provides access to a variety of constitutions, statutes, court opinions, law review articles, news articles, and other resources—including all Supreme Court decisions issued since 1893. Other useful sources of information include the U.S. Government Printing Office (*www.gpo.gov*), which contains a complete copy of the U.S. Code, and the Library of Congress's THOMAS system (*thomas.loc.gov*), which offers access to bills pending before Congress as well as recently passed laws. Of course, the Internet changes every second of every day, so it is best to do some independent searching. Most cases, studies, and opinions that are cited or referred to in public debate can be found online— and *everything* can be found in one library or another.

The Internet can provide a basic understanding of most important legal issues, but not all sources can be found there. To find some documents it is necessary to visit the law library of a university or a public law library; some cities have public law libraries, and many library systems keep legal documents at the main branch. On the following page are some common citation forms.

COMMON CITATION FORMS

Source of Law	Sample Citation	Notes
U.S. Supreme Court	*Employment Division* v. *Smith*, 485 U.S. 660 (1988)	The U.S. Reports is the official record of Supreme Court decisions. There is also an unofficial Supreme Court ("S. Ct.") reporter.
U.S. Court of Appeals	*United States* v. *Lambert*, 695 F.2d 536 (11th Cir.1983)	Appellate cases appear in the Federal Reporter, designated by "F." The 11th Circuit has jurisdiction in Alabama, Florida, and Georgia.
U.S. District Court	*Carillon Importers, Ltd.* v. *Frank Pesce Group, Inc.*, 913 F.Supp. 1559 (S.D.Fla.1996)	Federal trial-level decisions are reported in the Federal Supplement ("F. Supp."). Some states have multiple federal districts; this case originated in the Southern District of Florida.
U.S. Code	Thomas Jefferson Commemoration Commission Act, 36 U.S.C., §149 (2002)	Sometimes the popular names of legislation—names with which the public may be familiar—are included with the U.S. Code citation.
State Supreme Court	*Sterling* v. *Cupp*, 290 Ore. 611, 614, 625 P.2d 123, 126 (1981)	The Oregon Supreme Court decision is reported in both the state's reporter and the Pacific regional reporter.
State Statute	Pennsylvania Abortion Control Act of 1982, 18 Pa. Cons. Stat. 3203-3220 (1990)	States use many different citation formats for their statutes.

Abortion, 12, 14, 15, 17–18, 31, 37, 45, 60, 62, 65, 67, 106, 126–127
  components of, 25
  laws in the states, 26
  and privacy, 6, 107
  on right to choose, 16
  timeline, 91
Absolute Strangers, (movie), 21
Aka v. *Jefferson Hospital Association,* 48–49
Alcohol, 108
Alfred P. Murrah Federal Building, 73
Alzheimer's disease, 117
American Center for Law and Justice, (ACLJ), 44, 77
American Civil Liberties Union, (ACLU), 44
American College of Obstetricians and Gynecologists, (ACOG)
  on unwanted treatments, 94, 109
American Life League, 112
Anglo-American, 29–30
Aquinas, Thomas, (St.), 28, 29, 40
Aristotle, 40
Arkansas, 48, 49
Arthur, Joyce, 24, 33
Augustine, St., 40

Beckwith, Francis, 41, 46–47
Bioethics, 36, 41, 109, 122–123
Blackmun, Harry, (Justice), 24
  on the fetus, 25, 27
Blackstone, William, 27
Blood transfusion, 93

Bork, Robert, 25
Born alive rule, 29, 47, 48
Boston Globe, 126
Bradley, Gerard
  on a mother and death of her child, 71–72
  the UVVA, 78
Broderick, John, 20
Brown, 93–94
Bureau of Justice Statistics, 54
Bush, George W., 17, 30, 31, 36, 53, 75
Bush, Jeb, 31
  on fetal guardian, 96, 98
  on stem cell research, 118

California, 18, 70–71
  on funding stem cell research with State funds, 120–121
  on stem cell research, 118
California Stem Cell Research and Cures Act, 121
Cancer, 117
Canon Law, 22
Carder, Angela, 80, 92, 99
Casper, Monica, 31–33
Cell lines, 118, 119
Center for Bioethics and Human Dignity, 41
Cesarean section, (C-section), 31, 81, 82–83, 100, 110
  rise in, 92
  on women not wanting, 90, 92
Chan, Louise, 107

Charleston, SC, 83, 84, 106, 108
Common Law, 47, 48
Conception, 12, 34–37, 39, 47
Concerned Women for America, 101–102
Condon, Charles, 83
  on cocaine, 107
  cost of a crack baby, 104–105
  drug enforcement not racist, 108
Costello, Robert
  on pregnant women and cocaine use, 95
Crack babies, 83
Crack moms, 87
Criminal homicide and the fetus, 55
Cullins, Vanessa, 25

Daley, George, 119
Daniels, Cynthia, 87
  the fetus as second patient, 94
Dean, John
  on Supreme Court Justices, 125, 126
DeLay, Tom, 60
Department of Health and Human Services, 30, 31, 36
Diseases
  possibly helped by stem cell research, 117, 120
District of Columbia, 111
DNA, 24–25, 43
Doerflinger, Richard, 122
  the embryo, 120–121
  his position on stem cell research, 17–18
Dorf, Michael, 61–62

Dred Scott v. *Sandford*, 45, 46
Drugs, 83
  during pregnancy, 19, 99
Duden, Barbara, 27
Durham, Christine, (Chief Justice), 62–63, 64

Ectopic, 25
Embryo, 12–13, 15, 17, 43
  refers to, 14
Establishment Clause, 28

Family Research Council, 124–125
Farmer, Rebecca, 37
Feinstein, Dianne
  on stem cell research, 119
Feminists for Life of America, 73
Ferguson v. *City of Charleston*, 84, 106, 108
  dangers of cocaine use, 104
Fertility clinics, 117
Fetal Guardian, 95
  and controversial, 96
Fetal homicide, 52–67, 69, 76, 78, 127
Fetus, 12–13, 15, 17, 22–23, 43, 82–83
  meaning of, 14
  and second patient, 39
Findlaw's Writ, 61
Florida Appeals Court
  on fetal guardian, 98
Foster, Daniel
  and regulations on human embryos, 122–123

Foster, Serrin, 73, 75
  the unborn child, 76
Fourbier, Keith, 44
Fourteenth Amendment, 16, 24, 44–45, 61–62, 64, 126
Fourth Amendment, 84
Frozen embryos, 35
  legal status of, 35–36
  for medical research, 117
Fulcher, Juley, 52, 53–51

Gallagher, Maggie, 76–77
Gandy, Kim
  on fetal rights, 124
Gazzaniga, Michael
  on human embryos, 123–124
George, Robert P.
  on human embryos for research, 123
George Washington University Hospital, 80
Gift of Life, The, 40, 45
Giganti, Joseph, 112
Gilligan, Stacey, 85, 88
Glens Falls, NY, 85
Gomez-Lobo, Alfonso
  on human embryos for research, 123
Graham, Jennifer, 101, 112
  on childbirth, 110
Griswold, 28–29

Hadley, Janet, 28, 32
  on abortion, 33
Hard Choices, Lost Voices, (Judges), 34
Harvard Medical School, 119
Hatch, Orrin, 37, 70

Hoyas, Eugene, 43–44
Human embryos, 116–117, 120–127

Illinois, 93
In re: Brown, 93–94
In utero, 109
In vitro fertilization, (IVF), 35, 117

Jacobse, Johannes
  on the unborn child, 14–15
J. D. S., 113
  her case, 96–99
  guardian appointed, 114–115
Jehovah's Witness, 110–111
  reject transfusions, 93
Jewish faith, 22
John Paul II, (Pope), 39 40
Judges, Donald, 34–35

Kahn, Jeffrey, 36
Kentucky, 78–79
Kerry, John, 73, 76–77
Klein, Martin, 20, 21
Klein, Nancy, 20, 21
Knights of Columbus, 51

Laci and Conner's Law, 74
Lejeune, Jerome
  on frozen embryos, 118
Libertarians for Life, 50
Life, 21, 24, 25, 39
Lofgren, Zoe, 57–58, 60, 61, 71
Logli, Paul, 108
  drugs and pregnant women, 107

Loma Linda University Center for Christian Bioethics, 111
Lou Gehrig's disease, 117
Louisiana, 35

Madyun, Ayesha, 111
Making Women Pay: The Hidden Cost of Fetal Rights, (Roth), 16, 29
Maloney, Carolyn, 65–66
Marciniak, Tracy, 75
on single-victim law, 72–73
Maternal-fetal conflict, 94
McDonagh, Eileen
on abortion rights, 34
McKnight, Regina, 85, 89, 109
her cocaine use during pregnancy, 101
Mediate animation, 22, 23
Medical University of South Carolina, 83
on testing pregnant women for drugs, 106
Mental incompetence, (pregnant women)
appointed a legal guardian, 112–113
guardian makes medical decisions, 114
Miscarriage, 65–66, 79
Missouri, 28–29
Modesto, 11
Morgan, Lynn, 31–33
Motherhood Protection Act, 57, 71

National Abortion Rights Action League, (NARAL), 30, 60

National Advocate for Pregnant Women, (NAPW), 86–87
National Clearing House for Alcohol and Drug Information, 102–103
National Coalition Against Domestic Violence, 52
National Organization for Women, (NOW), 37, 61, 86
National Review, 110
New Oxford Review, The, 43
Newsweek, 12
New York Civil Liberties Union, (NYCLU), 85, 88

O'Connor, Sandra Day
on *Roe* v. *Wade*, 125
Oklahoma City bombing, 73
Orr, Robert
on blood transfusions, 111–112

Paltrow, Lynn, 86–87
women's rights on abortion, 89–90
Partial Birth Abortion Ban Act of 2003, 31
Pence, Mike, 46
Perkins, Tony
on rights of born and unborn, 124–125
Personhood, 22–23, 33, 39, 41, 44, 47, 50, 127
before birth, 19
embryo research, 122
Peterson, Connor, 10, 11, 12, 13, 73–74, 112
Peterson, Laci, 10, 11, 18, 112

Peterson, Scott, 10
complaint against, 13
and convicted, 11, 12, 13
the two counts of murder, 13
Planned Parenthood Federation of America, 25, 30
Pleus, Robert, (Judge)
on guardian for unborn child, 113–114
the unborn child, 12–14
Pregnant women
alcohol use, 102–103
laws regulating conduct of, 80–99
making medical decisions, 90
objections to testing for drugs and alcohol, 86
on seeking medical care, 89
on smoking, 102–103
and substance abuse, 83
threatening them with prosecution for drug use, 83–84, 106
President's Council on Bioethics
on human embryos, 122–123
Privacy, 107
Pro-choice, 12, 14, 30, 37, 41
and life begins at birth, 24
pregnant women and their rights, 95–99
on UVVA, 18–19
and women's rights, 30

Pro-life, 12, 16, 39, 40
  on embryo research,
    123
  life begins at concep-
    tion, 24, 33
  and new technology,
    51
  oppose stem cell
    research, 117
  rights of unborn
    child, 16–17
  on UVVA, 18–19
Protestant, 22–23

Rae, Scott, 109
  on C-sections, 110
Rehnquist, William, 125
  on viability, 50
Rocha, Sharon, 73–74,
  75
Roe v. Wade, 15, 21, 30,
  41, 44–45, 46, 47, 58,
  59, 61, 91, 98, 106
  on fetal rights, 124
  and fetus not a person,
    17, 22–23
  overturning of,
    125–126
  time of viability, 16
Roman Catholic, 23,
  117–118
  on life and conception,
    39–40
Ronald Reagan's "Person-
  hood Proclamation,"
  42
Roth, Rachel, 15, 16,
  29–30, 32 , 94, 95
  pregnant women and
    cocaine, 86, 87
Rowland, Melissa, 19,
  112
  and charged with
    murder of her
    stillborn, 100

Sacred Congregation
  for the Doctrine of
  the Faith, 40
San Francisco Bay, 10
Sekulow, Jay, 77
Sheldon, Lou, 109
Short, John, 20
Silent Scream, The,
  (film), 39
Single-victim laws,
  57–58, 60, 61
  do not serve justice,
    75
  a threat to abortion
    rights, 70–71
Smoking, 108, 109
South Carolina, 89
  fetus is a person, 105
  on prosecuting preg-
    nant women for
    cocaine use, 83–84,
    103, 104, 106
South Carolina Drug
  Prevalence Study,
  108
South Carolina Medical
  Association, (SCMA),
  88, 89
  on cocaine and preg-
    nancy, 87
South Carolina Supreme
  Court Upholds
  Conviction for
  Prenatal Cocaine
  Use, 105
Specter, Arlen
  and pro-choice,
    125–126
Stanislaus County, 13
State Children's Health
  Insurance Program,
  (SCHIP), 17, 18, 30,
  31, 49
  and covering unborn
    children, 120

State v. Gethers, 98
State v. Mc Knight, 86,
  87, 88, 89, 106
Stem cell research, 37,
  127
  on fetal rights laws,
    119
  finding cures for dis-
    eases, 117, 121
  funding of, 120, 121
  and reproducing
    human cells in
    laboratory, 116
Stevens, John Paul,
  (Justice), 28–29
  on testing pregnant
    women for drugs,
    84–85
Stillbirth, 17–18

Tennessee, 35
Thompson, Tommy,
  69
Traditional Values
  Coalition, 109

Unborn child, 14, 15
  guardian for,
    112–115
  legal debate over,
    127
  and legal protection,
    12, 115
  neglect of, 115
  on parents making
    Martyrs of, 111
  not recognized in law
    as persons, 23
Unborn victim laws,
  70
  affect on abortion,
    76–77
  on covering a child
    from conception,
    79

Unborn Victims of Violence Act, (UVVA), 18, 31, 49, 53, 56, 58, 60, 61, 65, 69, 72, 74, 120–121
and abortion, 76, 77
final language of, 78
on recognizing unborn victims, 75
and stem cell research, 120
United States Conference of Catholic Bishops position on stem cell research, 117–118
United States Congress, 15
law on murder of unborn child, 18
United States Constitution, 16

United States Supreme Court, 15, 16, 20–21, 24
University of Minnesota, 36
Unwanted medical care, 90–95, 99
Utah, 19, 37, 70
and fetal homicide laws, 62–63
Utero, 59–60

Viability, 41, 50, 107
and fetal homicide laws, 65
Violence against women, 54–55, 56, 66–67, 70

Walen, Alec, 64
Walker, John, 50
Watkins, William, 44

Webster v. *Reproductive Health Services*, 28, 47, 50, 51
Whitner, Cornelia, 105
Whitner v. *State*, 105
Whitney, Catherine, 21
on frozen embryos, 35
Whitney v. *State*, 89
Wisconsin, 69
Wixtrom, Jennifer, 98
Women's rights, 30–31
Wright, Wendy, 101–102

Young, Cathy
and abortion, 126, 127
fetal rights, 127
on UVVA, 126
Young v. *St. Vincent's Medical Center, Inc*, 98

Zygote, 14, 24–25, 40, 43, 57

page:
11: Associated Press/Turlock Journal/MartyBicek
26: Associated Press Graphics
59: Associated Press Graphics
91: Associated Press Graphics

Cover: © Cameron/CORBIS

ALAN MARZILLI, M.A., J.D., of Durham, North Carolina, is an independent consultant working on several ongoing projects for state and federal government agencies and nonprofit organizations. He has spoken about mental health issues in thirty states, the District of Columbia, and Puerto Rico; his work includes training mental health administrators, nonprofit management and staff, and people with mental illness and their family members on a wide variety of topics, including effective advocacy, community-based mental health services, and housing. He has written several handbooks and training curricula that are used nationally. He managed statewide and national mental health advocacy programs and worked for several public interest lobbying organizations in Washington, D.C., while studying law at Georgetown University.